Pronunciation Practice

The Sounds of North American English

Carol Burrill

PRO LINGUA ⬤ ASSOCIATES

Pro Lingua Associates, Publishers
P.O. Box 1348
Brattleboro, Vermont 05302 USA
Office: 802-257-7779
Orders: 800-366-4775
Email: info@ProLinguaAssociates.com
WebStore www.ProLinguaAssociates.com
SAN: 216-0579

*At Pro Lingua
our objective is to foster an approach
to learning and teaching that we call
interplay, the **inter**action of language
learners and teachers with their materials,
with the language and culture,
and with each other in active, creative
and productive **play**.*

This book was set by Arthur A. Burrows following the design by the author, who used Arial, a very common contemporary sans serif font of which there are a great many variations. It was developed to closely resemble other popular faces, some of which were under copyright; however, its curves and terminal strokes are somewhat more graceful than those of most of the earlier, industrial-style sans serifs. It is used here because its bold and italic faces are clear and distinctive and because it includes the phonetic symbols used in the book. The book was printed and bound by Gasch Printing, Odenton, Maryland. The cover design is by AA Burrows. The photographs used are from the Dreamstime.com agency: front cover © Dmitriy Cherevko; back cover, top © Maximino Gomes, center © Richard Thomas, bottom © Alexandr Frolov; cloth background © Graemo.

Printed in the United States of America
Second printing 2013.

Key to the Symbols
used in this book

Traditional Symbol or Name	International Phonetic Alphabet (IPA)	PLA Phonetic Alphabet	Key Words
short ă	/æ/	A	ask, thank
medium ä	/a/	AH	are, father
long ā	/eʸ/	AI	ate, make
schwa a	/ə/	uh	about, idea
b	/b/	B	big, job
soft c	/s/	S	city, dance
hard c	/k/	K	come, music
ch	/tʃ/	CH	child, much
d	/d/	D	do, need
short ĕ	/ɛ/	E	enjoy, best
long ē	/iʸ/	EE	eat, we
f	/f/	F	for, if
soft g	/dʒ/	J	gentle, age
hard g	/g/	G	good, big
h	/h/	H	happy, behind
short ĭ	/ɪ/	I	if, with
long ī	/aʸ/	AY	idea, tie
diphthong oi	/oʸ/	OY	oil, join
j	/dʒ/	J	just, enjoy
k	/k/	K	keep, back
l	/l/	L	look, school
m	/m/	M	make, time
n	/n/	N	no, fine
long n	/n̩/	N	didn't, sudden
ng	/ŋ/	NG	length, sing
short ŏ	/a/	AH	on, stop
long ō	/oʷ/	O	open, no
diphthong ou or ow	/æʷ/	OU	out, down, now

Key to the Symbols used in this book

schwa o	/ə/	UH	<u>o</u>f, l<u>o</u>ve
open ô	/ɔ/	OR	<u>or</u>, st<u>or</u>e
long o͞o	/uʷ/	OO	t<u>oo</u>l, t<u>oo</u>
short o͝o	/ʊ/	U	b<u>oo</u>k, g<u>oo</u>d
schwa oo	/ə/	UH	bl<u>oo</u>d, fl<u>oo</u>d
p	/p/	P	<u>p</u>ut, sto<u>p</u>
qu	/kw/	KW	<u>qu</u>ick, s<u>qu</u>are
r	/r/	R	<u>r</u>un, ca<u>r</u>
r-controlled vowels	/r̩/	ER	<u>ear</u>n, doct<u>or</u>
s	/s/	S	<u>s</u>o, ye<u>s</u>
sh	/ʃ/	SH	<u>sh</u>e, wi<u>sh</u>
s pronounced ZH	/ʒ/	ZH	televi<u>s</u>ion, u<u>s</u>ual
t	/t/	T	<u>t</u>en, pu<u>t</u>
soft th	/θ/	th	<u>th</u>ank, mon<u>th</u>
hard *th*	/ð/	TH	<u>th</u>is, smoo<u>th</u>
tapped t	/t̬/ or /ɾ/	D	ci<u>t</u>y, ma<u>tt</u>er
short ŭ	/ə/	UH	<u>u</u>p, r<u>u</u>n
medium u	/u/	OO	r<u>u</u>le, tr<u>u</u>e
long u	/yu/	YOO	<u>U</u>.S., val<u>ue</u>
v	/v/	V	<u>v</u>ery, gi<u>v</u>e
w	/w/	W	<u>w</u>ell, sho<u>w</u>
x	/ks/ or /gz/	KS or GZ	ne<u>x</u>t, e<u>x</u>ample
short y	/y/	Y	<u>y</u>ou, wa<u>y</u>
long y	/iʸ/	EE	eas<u>y</u>, ver<u>y</u>
z	/z/	Z	<u>z</u>oo, si<u>z</u>e

Note: *This book focuses on mastering the most frequently used words in North American English. Therefore, not every possible pronunciation of every alphabet letter appears here. Sound-to-letter correspondences that are infrequent in everyday speech are not included.*

Contents

Contents

Contents

Contents

Introduction

Pronunciation Practice is a workbook/CD set for teachers and students of English as a second or foreign language. It is intended for high-beginning to advanced students. It is a photocopyable book. Although the book can be used without the CDs, the accompanying CDs feature the sounds of North American English presented in authentic, natural pronunciation. The vocabulary is modeled in a clear, standard North American accent. The conversations include all the features of genuine connected speech. Therefore, the student has the opportunity to listen to and practice the individual sounds and the musical patterns of sentences (intonation and rhythm), the connections between words in a sentence (blending and linking), and the idiomatic shortcuts (reductions) of authentic North American speech. Although North American English refers to a variety of dialects spoken in the United States and Canada, there is a significant common core of pronunciation that distinguishes it from other varieties of English spoken around the world. This common core is reflected in this book and accompanying CDs. For purposes of consistency, the voices on the CDs speak a single widespread dialect of North American English: West Coast, USA.

This book with its CDs will help beginning students get the right start in pronunciation in the early stages of learning English. Intermediate and advanced students can improve the accuracy of their pronunciation and perfect their North American accent.

The complete package of five CDs is available as two different sets: three CDs for the Basic Lessons and two CDs for the listening component of the Appendix II activities – distinguishing and pronouncing contrasting pairs (often called minimal pairs).

Although the book may be used without the CDs, the Basic Lesson set includes conversations, which are more effective for the learner when spoken by different voices. Each of the Basic Lessons has two tracks. The "v track" includes the words (vocabulary) in the boxes. The "c track" is the conversation. On the second set of CDs, Contrasting Pairs, there is one track for each of the 24 one-page sets of activities – pages 84 to 107. Each page has five activities working with contrasting pairs.

This book and five CDs can be used for self-study. The book with or without the CDs can be used as the primary pronunciation tool in an ESL multi-skills class. It is also appropriate as a supplementary text in a conversation, speaking, or oral communication class. It is ideally used as an extension and additional practice of the concepts introduced in *Teaching North American English Pronunciation* by Raymond C. Clark and Richard Yorkey (2011 Pro Lingua Associates).

Features of This Book

- **The lessons are organized alphabetically.** This is the most sensible order for the majority of ESL learners and teachers. However, users of this text should feel free to reorder the lessons according to personal learning or teaching style.

- **The heading for each lesson includes the usual public school name for the target sound, a simplified International Phonetic Alphabet (IPA) symbol, and the Pro Lingua Associates (PLA) Phonetic Alphabet symbol**. Some students have experience, possibly through their children, with the language of phonics taught in American schools. But many students are more familiar with the IPA symbols that they may have studied in their own countries. The Pro Lingua Associates Phonetic Alphabet is used in *Teaching North American English Pronunciation.* It was developed to avoid diacritic marks and unfamiliar symbols. Accordingly, all of the sounds of English are represented with familiar alphabet letters. (See p. iii for a list and explanation of symbols.)

- **The choice of words with target sounds for each letter of the alphabet is based on lists of the most common words in English.** The 25 words (or fewer) at the top of each page come from frequency lists of both written and spoken English. Not all words in the English language are equally useful. By focusing on those words that students are most likely to use in normal conversation, students will quickly improve their overall oral intelligibility.

- **Each lesson includes target sounds in isolated words as well as in connected speech.** The vocabulary section of each lesson includes the target sound at the beginning, middle, and end positions within words. The conversation in each lesson allows further practice of the target sounds, using a sampling of the vocabulary words in connected speech.

- **Three appendices include interactive activities to reinforce the target sounds and words presented in each lesson.** They are *Expansion Activities*, *Contrasting Pairs*, and *Syllable Stress Flash Cards.*

- **There is a Glossary of pronunciation terms at the end of this book.**

**Special thanks
to Kate Burrill, Mark Burrill, Mason Roberts,
and my mentor teacher, Lynne Whitaker.**

short ă /æ/ A

initial	medial	
accident	bad	laugh
after	can	man
am	damage	matter
and	glass	ran
angry	had	stand
answer	happen	thank
as	happy	that
ask	have	understand
at		

CD One, track 1

Student A: What's the matter? You look angry.

Student B: I am. I had a car accident.

Student A: What happened?

Student B: A man ran a red light. He damaged my fender. And he broke the glass on my headlight.

Student A: That's too bad!

CD One, track 2

medium ä /a/ AH

initial	medial	
all	call	start
almost	car	talk
also	fall	walk
although	far	wall
always	farm	want
are	father	wash
art	hard	watch
autumn	large	water
	saw	

Note: *Speakers in many areas of North America will pronounce some of these words with the open ô /ɔ/ AW sound for the letter* **a**.

CD One, track 3

Student A: Where do you <u>want</u> to go for Thanksgiving this <u>autumn</u>?

Student B: I <u>almost</u> <u>always</u> visit my <u>father</u> on his <u>farm</u>.

Student A: Really? Is it <u>far</u>?

Student B: Yes. <u>Also</u>, it's <u>hard</u> to get there by <u>car</u>. <u>All</u> the roads <u>are</u> dirt.

CD One, track 4

long ā /eʸ/ AI

initial	medial	final
able	became	away
aid	explain	day
aim	gave	lay
ate	late	may
	main	say
	make	today
	place	way
	rain	
	space	
	table	
	wait	

CD One, track 5

Student A: Sorry I'm <u>late</u>! I can <u>explain</u>.

Student B: Don't worry. We'll <u>make</u> some <u>space</u> at the <u>table</u>. Here's a <u>place</u>.

Student A: I wasn't <u>able</u> to get a taxi because of the <u>rain</u>. Everyone was <u>waiting</u> for one <u>today</u>.

CD One, track 6

schwa a /ə/ uh

initial	medial		final
about	because	langu<u>age</u>	camer<u>a</u>
<u>a</u>gain	can*	man<u>age</u>	idea
ago	company	mess<u>age</u>	past<u>a</u>
amount	especially	prob<u>a</u>bly	
another	hospit<u>a</u>l	purch<u>a</u>se	
around	human	usu<u>a</u>l	
<u>a</u>ttach	husb<u>a</u>nd	wom<u>a</u>n	
<u>a</u>way			

*__Note:__ The pronunciation of **can** is usually reduced to /kən/ in the middle of a sentence.*

CD One, track 7

Worker A: My <u>manager</u> is in the <u>hospital</u>. I'd like to organize a gift. Any <u>ideas</u>?

Worker B: How <u>about</u> flowers? If everyone at the <u>company</u> agrees to give a small <u>amount</u> of money, you <u>can</u> <u>purchase</u> some <u>especially</u> nice ones.

Worker A: Great! And we <u>can</u> <u>attach</u> a get-well <u>message</u>. I'll send a memo <u>around</u> the office right <u>away</u>!

CD One, track 8

b /b/ B

	initial	medial	final
back	between	about	describe
ball	big	above	job
bath	boat	baby	
beautiful	books	remember	
because	box		
before	boys		
begin	building		
believe	but		
beside	buy		
better			

CD One, track 9

Wife: <u>Remember</u>, my sister and her twin <u>baby</u> <u>boys</u> are coming for the weekend.

Husband: You'd <u>better</u> <u>buy</u> some toys <u>before</u> they come.

Wife: I <u>believe</u> we still have <u>building</u> blocks, <u>balls</u>, and some <u>beautiful</u> picture <u>books</u> in the old toy <u>box</u>.

Husband: And we can put the toy <u>boat</u> <u>beside</u> the <u>bath</u>tub.

CD One, track 10

b /b/ B clusters

initial	medial	final
black	celebrate	able
blue	object*	responsible
bread	probably	table
break	problem	terrible
bridge	public	
bright	subject*	
bring		
brother		
brought		
brown		

***Note:** There are two pronunciations (and meanings) for each of these words. Stress on the last syllable is a verb (e.g., ob·JECT); stress on the first syllable is a noun (e.g., OB·ject).*

CD One, track 11

Student A: I want to <u>celebrate</u> my <u>brother</u>'s birthday at my house. Are you <u>able</u> to <u>bring</u> some wine and <u>bread</u>?

Student B: No <u>problem</u>. How about candles for the <u>table</u>?

Student A: I <u>probably</u> have some. But could you be <u>responsible</u> for the candles on the cake?

Student B: Sure. And while we're on the <u>subject</u> of candles, how old is he, anyway?

CD One, track 12

soft c /s/ S*

initial	medial	final
celebrate	ac<u>c</u>ept	dance
center	ac<u>c</u>ident	face
circle	can<u>c</u>el	force
citizen	con<u>c</u>ern	ice
city	decide	introduce
	excellent	once
	medicine	produce**
	officer	reduce
	receive	replace
	suc<u>c</u>eed	since

*Note: Normally, when the letter c is followed by e, i, or y, the pronunciation of c is /s/. If the letter c is followed by a, o, u, or a consonant, the pronunciation is usually /k/.

**Note: There are two pronunciations (and meanings) for this word. Stress on the last syllable is a verb (pro·DUCE); stress on the first syllable is a noun (PRO·duce).

CD One, track 13

Student A: I have to <u>face</u> an immigration <u>officer</u> today. I've got my <u>citizen</u>ship interview.

Student B: Don't be <u>concerned</u>! I'm sure you'll <u>succeed</u>. Let me drive you into the <u>city</u>.

Student A: Thanks! I <u>accept</u>. I've only been downtown <u>once</u> before.

Student B: It'll <u>reduce</u> your nervousness to have a friend with you. And when you <u>receive</u> your results, we can go out and <u>celebrate</u>!

CD One, track 14

hard c /k/ K*

	initial	medial	final
calm	copy	record**	public
care	correct	second	ethnic
carry	could	because	luck
cold	count	difficult	music
color	culture	document	
come	cure	education	
cook	cut	local	

*Note: The hard c at the beginning of a word or stressed syllable has more aspiration (air) than the hard c in an unstressed position in a word.

**Note: There are 2 pronunciations (and meanings) for this word. Stress on the last syllable is a verb (re·CORD); stress on the first syllable is a noun (RE·cord).

CD One, track 15

Student A: My teacher asked us to <u>cook</u> something from our own <u>culture</u> for the school potluck.

Student B: Is it <u>difficult</u> to find all the ingredients <u>locally</u>?

Student A: No, <u>because</u> Los Angeles has lots of <u>ethnic</u> markets.

Student B: I wish I <u>could</u> <u>come</u>. It sounds like an <u>education</u> in international <u>cooking</u>!

CD One, track 16

---

hard c /k/ K clusters

initial	medial	final
clean	include	contact
climb	democracy	correct
close*	increase**	expect
clothes	describe	fact
create	o'clock	
credit	direction	
crime	school	
cross	discover	
cry	welcome	

***Note:** There are two pronunciations (and meanings) for this word. /kloʷz/ means "to shut" and /kloʷs/ means "near."*

****Note:** There are two pronunciations (and meanings) for this word. Stress on the last syllable is a verb (in·CREASE); stress on the first syllable is a noun (IN·crease).*

CD One, track 17

Student A: I just <u>discovered</u> that my <u>credit</u> card number was stolen.

Student B: Oh no! Did your bank <u>contact</u> you?

Student A: Yes. They noticed a sudden <u>increase</u> in spending. Between 1 and 2 <u>o'clock</u> yesterday, somebody bought lots of <u>clothes</u> and <u>school</u> supplies, <u>including</u> a new computer.

Student B: They'll probably <u>create</u> a new account for you. They need to <u>close</u> your old account and report the <u>crime</u> to the police.

CD One, track 18

ch /tʃ/ CH

initial	medial	final	
change	achieve	attach	such
charge	purchase	each	teach
check		much	touch
choose		rich	watch
chance		speech	which
child		stretch	
children			

CD One, track 19

Student A: I'm having a hard time <u>choosing</u> a preschool for my <u>children</u>.

Student B: That's <u>such</u> a hard choice! You need to <u>check</u> to be sure the <u>teachers</u> are good.

Student A: That's true, but I have to think about how <u>much</u> they <u>charge</u>. I'm not <u>rich</u>!

Student B: We all need to <u>watch</u> <u>each</u> penny these days. Good luck deciding <u>which</u> school is best.

CD One, track 20

---

d /d/ D

initial	medial	final
date	already	good
days	idea	had
didn't	introduce	head
difficult	ready	made
do	study	need
done	suddenly	read*
down	today	road
during		said
		should
		would

Note: There are two pronunciations (and meanings) for this word. /rɛd/ is the past tense and /riʸd/ is the present tense.

CD One, track 21

Student A: You <u>said</u> you <u>would</u> <u>introduce</u> me to your cousin, <u>didn't</u> you?

Student B: Yes, of course! You <u>need</u> to start <u>dating</u>.

Student A: It's <u>difficult</u> for me, but I think I'm <u>ready</u>. It has <u>already</u> been a year since my wife died.

Student B: If you think it's a <u>good</u> idea, I'll call my cousin <u>today</u>.

CD One, track 22

short ĕ /ɛ/ E

initial	medial	
education	best	well
empty	get	went
end	left	when
enjoy	men	where
enter	never	yes
ever	read*	
every	ready	
except	their	
explain	them	
extra	very	

Note: *There are two pronunciations (and meanings) for this word. /riᵛd/ is the present tense and /rɛd/ is the past tense.*

CD One, track 23

Parent A: When do you think babies are <u>ready</u> to move into <u>their</u> own room?

Parent B: <u>Well</u>, I think you know <u>best</u>. But I <u>read</u> that in some cultures, children <u>never</u> <u>get</u> <u>their</u> own bedroom.

Parent A: Really? <u>Where</u>?

Parent B: In Nepal, for example, there isn't usually an <u>extra</u> room. It's the <u>exception</u> for children to have <u>their</u> own bedrooms.

CD One, track 24

long ē /iʸ/ EE

initial	medial		final
each	area	need	agree
easy	between	neither	be
eat	feel	please	me
either	green	read	see
even	idea	speak	the*
	keep	street	we
	means	these	

*Note:** Many people pronounce **the** with a long ē pronunciation /iʸ/ before vowels and the semivowel y. Before consonants, the schwa pronunciation /ə/ is usual.*

CD One, track 25

Wife: I think this <u>area</u> <u>between</u> the <u>street</u> and the house <u>needs</u> a tree.

Husband: I <u>agree</u>. You have a <u>green</u> thumb. <u>Please</u> put one in.

Wife: Should <u>we</u> <u>speak</u> to the landlord first?

Husband: Nah. I have a <u>feeling</u> he'll <u>be</u> <u>pleased</u> if we <u>keep</u> up <u>the</u> yard.

CD One, track 26

-ed endings*

/t/ T	/d/ D	/Id/ ID or /əd/ uhD
asked	covered	accepted
danced	cried	counted
dropped	filled	decided
laughed	happened	divided
walked	moved	ended
wished	turned	wanted

*Note: The –ed ending sounds like /t/ after a voiceless sound. It sounds like /d/ after a voiced sound. It sounds like /Id/ or /əd/ after a **d** or **t** sound.*

CD One, track 27

Wife: I <u>decided</u> to watch the *Titanic* DVD last night.

Husband: Again? You <u>wanted</u> to see it for the fifth time?

Wife: Yes. I <u>laughed</u> and <u>cried</u> just like the first time I saw it. That movie's <u>filled</u> with romance.

Husband: It never <u>moved</u> me. I guess it's a chick flick.

Wife: Maybe so. I <u>asked</u> my sister how many times she's seen it, and she <u>counted</u> ten times!

CD One, track 28

f /f/ F

initial		medial	final
far	first	before	half
feed	fix	carefully	if
feel	follow	difference	life
few	food	difficult	off
fight	for	officer	
fill	forget		
find	funny		
fine			

CD One, track 29

Student A: I have a <u>funny</u> <u>feel</u>ing someone is <u>follow</u>ing us.

Student B: It's a police <u>officer</u>. Pull <u>off</u> the road.

Student A: Oh, no! I've never been stopped <u>before</u>. This is the <u>first</u> time. What should I do?

Student B: He'll ask you to <u>find</u> a <u>few</u> things, like your license and registration. Speak to him politely and <u>carefully</u>. Maybe he'll let you <u>off</u> without a <u>fine</u>.

CD One, track 30

f /f/ F clusters

initial	medial	final
flag	afraid	gift
floor	after	himself
flowers	grandfather	left
fly	perfect	lift
free	wonderful	myself
fresh		soft
friend		
from		
fruit		

CD One, track 31

Brother: This party is the perfect gift for Grandfather's birthday!

Sister: Everything looks wonderful. The fruit bowls and the fresh flowers are on the table. I washed the floor and all the windows myself.

Brother: His best friends from San Francisco will fly in this afternoon. There's nothing left to do!

CD One, track 32

soft g /dʒ/ J*

initial	medial	final	
general	budget	age	huge
gentle	imagine	average	judge
giant	intelligent	bridge	language
	region	college	manage
	vegetables	damage	message
	wages	edge	

*Note: Normally, when the letter **g** is followed by **e**, **i**, or **y**, the pronunciation of **g** is /dʒ/. If the letter **g** is followed by **a**, **o**, **u**, or a consonant, the pronunciation is usually /g/.*

CD One, track 33

Husband: Look at this huge credit card bill! We need to manage our money better.

Wife: How do you imagine we can save money? Our wages are low and the kids' college expenses are high.

Husband: We have to make a strict budget. It's too hard always living on the edge!

CD One, track 34

hard g /g/ G

initial	medial	final
gas	again	big
games	against	drug
get	ago	egg
girl	begin	flag
give	forget	leg
go	forgive	
goes	magazine	
good	organize	
got	together	
guess		
guy		

CD One, track 35

Employee A: Can you help me <u>organize</u> some <u>games</u> for the company picnic?

Employee B: I <u>guess</u>. But don't <u>forget</u> how everyone <u>got</u> mad last time.

Employee A: <u>Give</u> me a break! That was a year <u>ago</u>. Now I know mixing <u>guys</u> and <u>girls</u> <u>together</u> for the "Three-<u>Legged</u> Race" is not a <u>good</u> idea.

Employee B: That's right. We don't want any sprained ankles <u>again</u> this year.

CD One, track 36

hard g /g/ G clusters

initial	medial
glad	agree
glass	angry
grandfather	argue
great	degree
green	forget
ground	forgive
group	paragraph
grow	program
	progress*
	regret
	suggest

***Note:** There are 2 pronunciations (and meanings) for this word. Stress on the last syllable is a verb (pro·GRESS); stress on the first syllable is a noun (PRO·gress).*

CD One, track 37

Husband: I'm sorry I <u>argued</u> with you. Are you ready to <u>forgive</u> and <u>forget</u>?

Wife: Sure. I'm <u>glad</u> we can a<u>gree</u> to disa<u>gree</u>.

Husband: I really re<u>gret</u> getting so <u>angry</u>. I'll try to <u>grow</u> up!

CD One, track 38

silent gh

medial		final
bright	might	high
brought	night	weigh
daughter	ought	through
eight	right	though
fight	straight	
light	thought	

CD One, track 39

Neighbor A: I thought you might like these tomatoes. They're straight from my garden.

Neighbor B: You're right. I love tomatoes. And the zucchinis you brought me last night were delicious! You ought to sell them at the Farmer's Market.

Neighbor A: No, I'm 75 years old and I'm through working. Though I do like gardening!

CD One, track 40

h /h/ H

initial		medial
had	hear	alcohol
half	help	behave
happen	her	behind
happy	here	
hard	him	
has	his	
hate	home	
have	hope	
he	how	
head	however	
health	hurry	

CD One, track 41

Student A: I <u>hope</u> Sam is not planning to drive <u>home</u> on <u>his</u> own. <u>He</u> <u>has</u> <u>had</u> too much <u>alcohol</u>.

Student B: <u>He</u> is <u>behaving</u> badly. <u>He</u> shouldn't get <u>behind</u> the wheel of any vehicle.

Student A: I <u>hate</u> to <u>have</u> to talk to <u>him</u>. <u>However</u>, if we don't <u>help</u> <u>him</u> get <u>home</u>, something terrible could <u>happen</u>.

CD One, track 42

short ĭ /I/ I

initial	medial	
if	admit	visit
in	sit	little
instead	give	will
invite	six	difficult
is	big	miss
it	thing	discuss
its/it's	bring	winter
	this	wish
	children	during
	contribute	since
	listen	with

CD One, track 43

Grandmother: <u>Listen</u>, <u>it's</u> time to <u>sit</u> down and <u>discuss</u> some<u>thing</u>. We should go <u>visit</u> the <u>children</u> <u>this</u> <u>winter</u>.

Grandfather: Why don't we <u>invite</u> them here <u>instead</u>? <u>Since</u> their house <u>is</u> so <u>little</u>, <u>it's</u> <u>difficult</u> to stay <u>with</u> them.

Grandmother: I <u>admit</u> our house <u>is</u> <u>big</u>ger. Let's tell them we <u>miss</u> them, and we <u>will</u> <u>contribute</u> to plane tickets to come here <u>during</u> Christmas.

Grandfather: I sure <u>wish</u> they would <u>bring</u> the grandkids <u>with</u> them, too!

CD One, track 44

long ī /aʸ/ AY

initial	medial		final
I	behind	like	die
idea	child	might	lie
island	decide	mind	tie
item	design	nice	
	diet	quiet	
	find	realize	
	high	right/write	
	kind	surprise	
	life	wife	

CD One, track 45

Husband: I just <u>realized</u> it's my <u>wife's</u> birthday. I can't <u>decide</u> how to <u>surprise</u> her.

Friend: Chocolates are a <u>nice</u> <u>idea</u>, if she's not on a <u>diet</u>. My <u>wife</u> <u>likes</u> <u>designer</u> candy.

Husband: This is her 40th, so I <u>might</u> need to <u>find</u> something with a <u>higher</u> price tag!

CD One, track 46

letter i special pronunciations

i pronounced like ē /iʸ/ EE	diphthong oi /oʸ/ OY
machine	avoid
magazine	boil
material	join
movie	noise
radio	oil
serious	point
	poison
	voice

CD Two, track 1

Student A: Will you <u>join</u> us and sign this petition? We want the President to hear the <u>voice</u> of parents.

Student B: What's the main <u>point</u> of your petition?

Student A: We believe there is too much adult <u>material</u> in the media. Our children can't <u>avoid</u> the sex and violence. It's on the internet, in <u>magazines</u>, in <u>movies</u>, and on the <u>radio</u>.

Student B: I agree; that's a <u>serious</u> problem.

CD Two, track 2

j /dʒ/ J

initial	medial
jail	enjoy
job	hijack
join	injure
joke	major
joy	majority
judge	object*
jump	project*
jury	reject*
just	subject*

Note: *There are 2 pronunciations (and meanings) for each of these words. Stress on the last syllable is a verb (e.g., ob·JECT); stress on the first syllable is a noun (e.g., OB·ject).*

CD Two, track 3

Student A: I just heard there was a hijacking on a major airline.

Student B: Really? Was anyone injured?

Student A: No, the hijacker was quickly arrested. Now he'll need to go before a judge and jury. He'll probably go to jail.

CD Two, track 4

k /k/ K*

initial	final	
keep	back	make
key	break	pick
kick	check	rock
kid	earthquake	shake
kill	joke	sick
kind	leak	speak
kiss	like	take
	look	talk
	luck	weak/week

***Note:** The /k/ at the beginning of a word or stressed syllable has more aspiration (air) than the /k/ in an unstressed position in a word.*

CD Two, track 5

Student A: How are you? You <u>look</u> <u>kind</u> of <u>sick</u>.

Student B: I do feel <u>weak</u>. And I'm <u>shaking</u> with chills.

Student A: You'd better <u>make</u> an appointment to <u>talk</u> with your doctor. He'll probably <u>take</u> you right away for a <u>check</u>-up.

CD Two, track 6

k /k/ K clusters

initial	medial	final
skill	blanket	ask
skin	likely	dark
sky	market	drink
	quickly	milk
	sickness	shrink
		sink
		thank
		think
		work

Note: *When the letter "k" is followed by an "n," the "k" is usually silent, as in <u>knee</u>, <u>knife</u>, <u>knock</u>, <u>know</u>, and <u>knowledge</u>.*

CD Two, track 7

Wife: I hate to <u>ask</u>, but could you go to the <u>market</u> for some <u>milk</u>? We don't have anything for the kids to <u>drink</u>.

Husband: Sure. I <u>think</u> I'm finished with this yard <u>work</u> anyway.

Wife: <u>Thanks</u>. Take a coat. The <u>sky</u> is getting <u>dark</u> and rain seems <u>likely</u>.

CD Two, track 8

l /l/ L

initial	medial	final
later	always	all
learn	believe	call
leave	dollar	cell/sell
left	excellent	school
like	follow	steal
listen		tell
live*		until
look		well
lost		will
love		
luck		

Note: The l is silent in several high-frequency words such as **could**, **should**, **talk**, **would**, *and* **walk**.

Note: There are two pronunciations (and meanings) for this word. /laʸv/ is an adjective meaning "not dead;" /lɪv/ is a verb meaning "to be alive" or "to make a home someplace."

CD Two, track 9

Student A: What bad luck! I lost my purse. I left it at my desk at school. When I went back later, it was gone.

Student B: Who would steal it? I believe you will find it. Have you called the school and talked with the office?

Student A: Not yet. I always keep my cell in my purse. Could I use yours?

CD Two, track 10

I /l/ L clusters

medial		final*
almost	o'clock	able
already	only	circle
also	plan	example
although	play	final
build	please	little
child	problem	middle
difficult	sleep	people
explain	unless	terrible
		trouble

Note: These final l's are long, forming a syllable on their own.

CD Two, track 11

Boss (on phone): What's the problem? It's already
11 o'clock!

Employee: I can explain. I had trouble sleeping. The
people next door were playing their music until
the middle of the night.

Boss: Please! That's a terrible excuse. Unless you're
able to get here by 12 o'clock, you'd better plan
on getting a new job!

CD Two, track 12

m /m/ M

initial	medial	final
make	family	am
man	promise	become
many	remember	come
me	woman	from
meet	women	mom
men		problem
might		some
minute*		them
more		time
movie		
my		

Note: *There are two pronunciations (and meanings) for this word. Stress on the second syllable (min·UTE) means "very small." Stress on the first syllable (MIN·ute) means "60 seconds."*

CD Two, track 13

Husband: <u>Come</u> on! It's almost <u>time</u> for the <u>movie</u> to start.

Wife: Give <u>me</u> a <u>minute</u>. I'm having a <u>problem</u> with <u>my</u> <u>make</u>-up.

Husband: OK, but <u>remember</u> we <u>promised</u> to <u>meet</u> your <u>mom</u> at the <u>movie</u> theater. She <u>might</u> <u>become</u> worried if we're late.

CD Two, track 14

m /m/ M clusters

medial	final
almost	arm
computer	calm*
empty	farm
example	film
government	form
grandmother	palm*
himself	storm
important	warm
improve	
number	
small	
something	

*Note: *The **l** in these words may also be silent. (E.g., **calm** may be pronounced /kalm/ or /kam/.)*

CD Two, track 15

Student A: The refrigerator's <u>almost</u> <u>empty</u>. How about we pick <u>something</u> up for dinner?

Student B: In this <u>storm</u>? Let's wait until it <u>calms</u> down.

Student A: The <u>computer</u> says the weather won't <u>improve</u> tonight. I guess we can <u>warm</u> up that <u>small</u> can of chili.

CD Two, track 16

---

n /n/ N

initial	medial	final	
need	another	again	in
never	any	can	mean
new	cannot	citizen	one
no	finally	done	question
nobody	finish	down	ten
now	many	explain	when
		fine	

CD Two, track 17

Student A: When do you have your citizenship interview?

Student B: In another week. I've been trying to finish studying the *100 Questions*. I also need to write down all the vocabulary words for the citizenship reading and writing tests.

Student A: You'll do fine! There are only ten questions from the *100 Questions*. And if you cannot understand what they mean, you can ask the examiner to explain.

CD two, track 18

---

n /n/ N clusters

medial	final	
answer	and	husband
country	around	learn
inside	can't	once
morning	chance	return
only	change	since
under	earn	stand
understand	find	turn
until	friend	want

CD Two, track 19

Student A: I <u>want</u> to look <u>around</u> for a new job. I need to <u>earn</u> more.

Student B: What do you think you can <u>find</u>? <u>Since</u> the economy is bad, it's hard to <u>change</u> jobs.

Student A: My <u>husband</u>'s <u>friend</u> told me he <u>learned</u> about computers at adult school. I'm going to study in the <u>mornings</u>. I think I'll <u>stand</u> a good <u>chance</u> of <u>finding</u> a new job <u>once</u> I <u>understand</u> more about computers.

CD Two, track 20

long n /n̩ / N*

medial	final
couldn't didn't sentence suddenly	cotton eaten frighten happen listen mountain often

__Note:__ In each of these words, the __n__ is long. In relaxed conversation, any preceding vowel will be silent. (E.g., __suddenly__ is pronounced /sədn̩liʲ/, not /sədənliʲ/.)

CD Two, track 21

Student A: Are you flying home to the Rocky Mountains?

Student B: No, I'm driving. Last time I got on a plane, I suddenly felt frightened. I couldn't take the flight.

Student A: Really? Does that happen often?

Student B: No. I didn't have any problems until this year.

CD Two, track 22

---

ng /ŋ/ NG

medial*	final	
length strength Washington	along among anything being belong bring hang long	morning nothing sing something strong thing young

Note: *Sometimes, when "ng" occurs in the middle of the root or stem of a word, the pronunciation is /ŋg/, as in E<u>ng</u>lish, a<u>ng</u>er, hu<u>ng</u>er, or si<u>ng</u>le.*

CD Two, track 23

Wife: Should I <u>bring</u> <u>along</u> a coat on our trip to <u>Washington</u>?

Husband: Definitely. The nights are <u>long</u> and cold at this time of year. <u>Bring</u> <u>something</u> warm.

Wife: I don't have <u>anything</u> full <u>length</u>. But here's <u>something</u> <u>hanging</u> in the closet that <u>belong</u>s to Mom. It looks like the perfect <u>thing</u> for winter weather.

CD Two, track 24

short ŏ /a/ AH*

initial	medial	
off	across	job
often	along	Los Angeles
on	borrow	not
opposite	bought	possible
ought	brought	probably
	cost	problem
	doctor	stop
	dollar	thought
	gone	tomorrow
	got	wrong

*Note: Speakers in many areas of the United States will pronounce some of these words with the open ô /ɔ/ AW sound for the letter o.

CD Two, track 25

Student A: Could I borrow a few dollars for gas? I got a new job. It starts tomorrow.

Student B: Not a problem. You ought to be on time on the first day!

Student A: Thanks. It probably costs less to take the bus across town. But I don't want to get on the wrong bus or get off at the wrong stop. Not on my first day.

CD Two, track 26

long ō /oʷ/ O

initial	medial	final
old	both	ago
only	close*	also
open	clothes	go
over	don't	know/no
owe/oh	goes	low
own	hope	slow
	nowhere	so
	phone	yellow
	those	

Note: There are two pronunciations (and meanings) for this word. /kloʷz/ means "to shut" and /kloʷs/ means "near."

CD Two, track 27

Wife: <u>Slow</u> down! Let's park <u>over</u> there, between <u>those</u> <u>yellow</u> posts.

Husband: <u>Those</u> spaces are <u>only</u> for handicapped drivers. <u>Both</u> of them. There's <u>nowhere</u> in this lot to park.

Wife: <u>Oh</u> <u>no</u>! I <u>hope</u> they <u>don't</u> start eating. We should have been here an hour <u>ago</u>.

Husband: I <u>know</u>. Why <u>don't</u> you <u>phone</u> them? I'll <u>go</u> to the <u>lower</u> parking level.

CD Two, track 28

---

ou and ow pronounced /æ^w/ OU

initial	medial		final
our	about	loud	how
out	amount	mountain	now
	around	noun	
	crowd	south	
	down	thousand	
	flower	town	
	hours	vowel	
	house		

CD Two, track 29

Husband: It's about time we think about buying a house in the mountains.

Wife: Fine with me. This downtown area is dirty, loud, and crowded. How much will it cost to move out of the city?

Husband: If we downsize to a small cabin, we can save around ten thousand every year.

Wife: Great! How about we move out now?

CD Two, track 30

schwa o /ə/ UH

initial	medial	
of	above	enough
once*	among	from
one*	another	love
other	brother	money
	color	month
	come	mother
	country	nothing
	cover	some
	does	wonderful
	done	

*Note: These words both start with the semivowel /w/. (E.g., **once** is pronounced /wəns/.)

CD Two, track 31

Student A: What's more important to you, love or money?

Student B: Definitely money, above all.

Student A: Really? How come?

Student B: Well, love doesn't cover your rent every month. But if you're rich, life is wonderful. Plus, if you have enough money, everyone loves you!

CD Two, track 32

open ô /ɔ/ OR

initial	medial	
or	before	poor
order	door	report
	for	short
	important	sport
	more	store
	morning	story

CD Two, track 33

Wife: Could you go to the store for a few things?
I need milk and eggs before I can start making
breakfast.

Husband: Sure. In just a minute. I'm reading an
important report in the morning paper. It says
that poor people in our city pay more for their
food than rich people.

Wife: Why is that?

Husband: Fewer stores want to open in poor
neighborhoods. This story says that in order to
keep prices lower, you need competition. Stores
can charge higher prices in poor areas.

CD Two, track 34

Three pronunciations for oo

long o͞o /uʷ/ OO	short o͝o /ʊ/ U	schwa oo /ə/ UH
choose cool moon noon room school soon too zoo	book cook good look stood wood	blood flood

CD Two, track 35

Daughter: Cool! Look at the full moon!

Mother: That brings back a flood of memories. Your
father and I stood right here and looked at that
same moon. We were in high school, like you.

Daughter: You have a good memory. That was a long
time ago!

Mother: Yes, but time flies. And I became old too soon!

CD Two, track 36

---

p /p/ P*

initial	medial	final
paper	appear	Europe
paragraph	capital	group
party	happen	hope
past	happy	keep
people	open	sleep
period	repeat	stop
poor	report	top
pull		up
push		
put		

*Note: The **p** at the beginning of a word or stressed syllable has more aspiration (air) than the **p** in an unstressed position in a word.*

CD Two, track 37

Student 1: A group of us are going to stop by the party at Paula's. Want to come?

Student 2: I can't. I have a report due first period tomorrow. I have to write a paragraph on each of the major capitals of Europe.

Student 1: Poor guy! If you happen to finish your paper, drop by later. People will be there past midnight.

CD Two, track 38

p /p/ P clusters*

initial	medial		final
play	apply	experience	help
please	computer	explain	jump
prefer	employ	important	
problem	empty	improve	
probably	especially	perhaps	
price	except	speak	
prepare	expect	spend	
pronounce			

*Note: The **p** at the beginning of a word or stressed syllable has more aspiration (air) than the **p** in an unstressed position in a word.*

CD Two, track 39

Student 1: My boss says he needs <u>help</u> at his office. Why don't you <u>apply</u>?

Student 2: I don't know. You <u>probably</u> have to <u>speak</u> English fluently.

Student 1: No <u>problem</u>. I'm pretty sure he <u>prefers</u> applications from people with <u>computer</u> skills. <u>Pronouncing</u> perfectly is not <u>especially</u> important for this job.

Student 2: Well, I have plenty of <u>computer</u> experience. And if he <u>employs</u> me, maybe my English will <u>improve</u> on the job!

CD Two, track 40

 Pronunciation Practice © 2013 by Carol Burrill • **43**

qu /kw/ KW*

initial	medial
quality	earthquake
quarter	equal
question	equipment
quick	liquid
quiet	request
quit	require
quite	square
quiz	
quote	

Note: *The /k/ sound at the beginning of a word or stressed syllable has more aspiration (air) than the /k/ in an unstressed position in a word.*

CD Two, track 41

Customer: I'd like to return this sports <u>equipment</u>.

Cashier: Is there a problem with the <u>quality</u>?

Customer: No, but it's not <u>quite</u> what I wanted for my birthday. I <u>quit</u> playing sports when I was a child.

Cashier: Of course. We just have one <u>request</u>: Please fill out this <u>questionnaire</u> about the return. Then go ahead and choose anything of <u>equal</u> or greater value in our store.

CD Two, track 42

r /r/ R

initial	medial	final
ready	around	are
real	arrive	before
relax	borrow	car
return	careful	for
right/write	carry	hair
room	period	there/their/they're
run	tomorrow	wear/where
	very	year
		your/you're

CD Two, track 43

Mother: <u>Your</u> <u>hair</u> needs cutting. Let's go <u>tomorrow</u>.

Son: No! Last time she chased me <u>around</u> the <u>room</u>. Then she <u>really</u> cut off a lot!

Mother: I'm sure she'll be <u>very</u> <u>careful</u> this time. If you <u>relax</u> and don't <u>run</u> away, you'll be done <u>before</u> you know it.

Son: I want to <u>wear</u> my <u>hair</u> long. I won't go <u>there</u>. <u>Period</u>!

CD Two, track 44

r-controlled vowels /r̩/ ER*

initial	medial	final
early earn	first girl learn perfect** person understand verb wonderful word work worry yesterday	another better doctor dollar Mr. never remember sir sure teacher together

*__Note:__ The vowel or vowels are silent before the long __r__ in each of these words. (E.g., __earn__ is pronounced /r̩n/; __doctor__ is pronounced /daktr̩/.)

**__Note:__ There are two pronunciations (and meanings) for this word. Stress on the last syllable is a verb (per·FECT); stress on the first syllable is an adjective (PER·fect).

CD Two, track 45

Student 1: Yesterday, Mr. Carter gave us a long list of irregular verbs to learn. I'll never remember all those words!

Student 2: Don't worry. I'm sure your teacher doesn't expect you to be perfect. Let's work together.

Student 1: That would be wonderful! I'll understand better if I work with another person.

CD Two, track 46

r /r/ R clusters

initial cluster		medial cluster	final cluster
break	price	already	hard
drive	probably	argue	north
free	promise	children	start
from	spring	different	tired
great	through	extra	warm
present*	true	important	
pretty	try		

*Note: *There are two pronunciations (and meanings) for this word. Stress on the last syllable is a verb (pre·SENT); stress on the first syllable is a noun (PRE·sent).*

CD Three, track 1

Student 1: I'll probably travel north to Portland this spring break. My children will be free.

Student 2: Great! Will you drive?

Student 1: I'm pretty sure. With the high price of flying, I'm going to try to go by car.

Student 2: But it's hard to travel with small children when they get tired.

Student 1: True, but I promised them a nice present if they don't argue.

CD Three, track 2

s /s/ S

initial	medial	final
said	beside	across
saw	listen	house
say	message	kiss
see	necessary	miss
seem	possible	this
seven		us
sick		yes
sing		
sister		
six		
so		
some		
soon		

CD Three, track 3

Wife: Have you <u>listened</u> to our phone <u>messages</u>?

Husband: Yeah. Your <u>sister</u> <u>said</u> she'll <u>see</u> us at your mom's <u>house</u>. Sid <u>says</u> <u>yes</u>, he wouldn't <u>miss</u> it. Sue is <u>sick</u>, <u>so</u> she <u>says</u> to give your mom a <u>kiss</u> for her.

Wife: Is it <u>possible</u> that Mom's really turning <u>seventy-six</u>? She <u>seemed</u> happy that <u>so</u> many of <u>us</u> will be there to <u>sing</u> "Happy Birthday."

CD Three, track 4

s /s/ S clusters

initial	medial	final
sky	answer	against
sleep	distance	almost
small	especially	ask
smoke	question	best
snow	understand	cost
special		forest
start		honest
stay		just
still		must
strong		trust

CD Three, track 5

Student 1: Honestly, I can't understand why I trusted you. I thought you could lead us through this forest. It's starting to snow and we're still a long distance from Stan's cabin.

Student 2: Stay calm. Look at the smoke in the sky! It must be from the cabin. We're almost there.

Student 1: Just in time! I need a strong drink and some sleep!

CD Three, track 6

s pronounced /z/ Z

medial		final	
business	prison	advise	his
busy	reason	always	is
easy	result	as	lose
husband	visit	because	raise
present		close*	these
president		clothes	use*
		excuse*	was
			wise

***Note:** The **s** in these words is pronounced /z/ in the verb form. When these words act as a noun, adjective, or adverb, the **s** is pronounced /s/.*

CD Three, track 7

Employee 1: Did you have your meeting with the president? Did you ask for a raise?

Employee 2: No. He was too busy. Say, do you think it's wise for me to give the reason I need a raise? It's not easy for me to admit that my husband is in prison!

Employee 1: I advise against it. It's none of their business. You deserve a raise because you always work hard and you get good results!

CD Three, track 8

---

other s pronunciations

sh pronounced /ʃ/ SH		su pronounced /ʃ/ SH	su and si pronounced /ʒ/ ZH
crash	she	issue	decision
English	shoe	sugar	measure
finish	should	sure	pleasure
fresh	show		television
push	shut		treasure
shape	wash		usual
share	wish		version

CD Three, track 9

Roommate 1: You should turn off the television and study your English.

Roommate 2: This show is almost finished. Anyway, it's in English, so don't make an issue of it.

Roommate 1: Sure. It's your decision. But if you want to be in shape for your exam tomorrow, you need to push yourself to study.

CD Three, track 10

-s endings*

/s/[1]	/z/[2]		/ Iz/ or /əz/[3]
its/it's	countries	needs	causes
makes	does	news	inches
minutes	eyes	problems	wages
rights	friends	questions	
states	goes	says	
	hours	towards	
	means	yours	

***Note: -s** endings (including plurals, possessives, and 3rd-person singular present tense) have three pronunciations, depending on the last sound in the root word:*

[1]**/s/** *pronunciation is after voiceless sounds*
[2]**/z/** *pronunciation is after voiced sounds*
[3]**/Iz/** or **/əz/** *pronunciation is after sounds usually spelled -ch, -sh, -s, -z, -ge/-dge*

CD Three, track 11

Wife: It <u>says</u> in the <u>news</u> that most of the <u>state's</u> workers will need to take a cut in <u>wages</u>.

Husband: That raises <u>questions</u>. <u>Does</u> that mean <u>yours</u> and mine? I think it just <u>means</u> government workers' <u>wages</u>.

Wife: That's right. Nearly every worker <u>needs</u> to have his <u>hours</u> reduced. Our state has big financial <u>problems</u>!

CD Three, track 12

t /t/ T*

initial		medial	final	
talk	time	attach	about	let
teach	to/too/two	between	at	might
telephone	tomorrow	protect	front	out
tell	tonight	return	great	put
ten	turn		hate	sit
			it	

Note: The /t/ at the beginning of a word or stressed syllable has more aspiration (air) than the /t/ in an unstressed position in a word.

CD Three, track 13

Child: Tomorrow it's my turn for Show and Tell.

Father: Great! What time do you talk? I'll come and sit in the front row.

Child: About ten o'clock. Can you bring Tommy? I want to teach the kids all about tarantulas.

Father: Well…. Let me telephone the teacher tonight to see if it's OK. Some kids might hate Tommy the tarantula.

CD Three, track 14

---

t /t/ T clusters*

initial	medial	final
travel	after	against
trip	country	almost
trouble	interest	best
true	into	doesn't
try	its/it's	expect
	sometime	fast
	start	just
	states	next
	stop	rest
	until	short

***Note**: The /t/ at the beginning of a word or stressed syllable has more aspiration (air) than the /t/ in an unstressed position in a word.*

CD Three, track 15

Student 1: Have any <u>interest</u> in taking a road <u>trip</u> across the United <u>States</u>? It's my brother's wedding and I'm the <u>best</u> man.

Student 2: <u>Doesn't</u> he live in Vermont? This is <u>short</u> notice, but I'd love to <u>travel</u> across the <u>country</u>.

Student 1: Great! We'll <u>start</u> tomorrow. I <u>expect</u> we'll drive <u>fast</u>, make <u>just</u> a few <u>rest</u> <u>stops</u>, and get there <u>sometime</u> on Friday.

CD Three, track 16

soft th /θ/ th

initial	medial	final
thank	anything	both
theater	healthy	earth
thing	nothing	length
think	something	month
thought	without*	north
through		south
throw		with*
		worth

Note: *the words* **with** *and* **without** *can be pronounced with either the hard or soft* **th** *pronunciation.*

CD Three, track 17

Employee A: <u>Thank</u> you for the ride home.

Employee B: <u>Think</u> <u>nothing</u> of it. We're <u>through</u> work at the same time. And we <u>both</u> live in the <u>north</u> part of town.

Employee A: I'll be <u>without</u> a car just this <u>month</u>. I <u>thought</u> I'd buy <u>something</u> used next <u>month</u>.

CD Three, track 18

hard *th* /ð/ TH

initial	medial	final
than	although	breathe
that	another	smooth
the	either	with*
their/there	father	
them	mother	
then	neither	
therefore	other	
this	together	
though	weather/whether	
	without*	

*Note: The words **with** and **without** can be pronounced with either the hard or soft **th** pronunciation.

CD Three, track 19

Student A: Would your mother and father rather live with you or in a retirement community?

Student B: Neither. They want to live together in their own house. And this is even though they are in their 80s!

Student A: Well, I wish them another 80 years of good health!

CD Three, track 20

special *t* pronunciations

silent t	ti sounds like /ʃ/ SH	t sounds like /tʃ/ CH
fasten listen often	action condition education information international mention* patient population position station	actually century culture future natural picture situation*

Note: When **t** follows **n**, as in **mention**, it is commonly pronounced **CH**. **Situation** has two **t**'s, the first in pronounced **CH**, the second **SH**.

CD Three, track 21

Student A: What do you think life will be like a <u>century</u> into the <u>future</u>?

Student B: I'm afraid the <u>situation</u> will be bad. We need to take <u>action</u> now on over<u>population</u>.

Student A: I agree. My <u>position</u> is that <u>international</u> <u>education</u> on birth control is necessary. Humans are a strain on the <u>natural</u> world.

CD Three, track 22

---

tapped t /t̬/ or /ɾ/ D*

medial	
beautiful	later
better	little
city	matter
community	notice
computer	pretty
daughter	security
duty	water
hospital	

Note: *When an unstressed -t- or -tt- is between vowel sounds, it becomes a quickly "tapped" **d** sound.*

CD Three, track 23

Neighbor 1: I <u>notice</u> your <u>daughter</u> leaves for work <u>pretty</u> late.

Neighbor 2: Yes. She's on <u>duty</u> at <u>Community</u> Hospital in the evenings. She works at the <u>security</u> desk.

Neighbor 1: It's lucky for her that the traffic is a <u>little</u> <u>better</u> going into the <u>city</u> <u>later</u> at night.

CD Three, track 24

---

short ŭ /ə/ UH

initial	medial	
under	but	result
understand	cut	run
unless	difficult	shut
until	discuss	study
up	just	succeed
upon	much	such
us	must	suddenly
		suffer

CD Three, track 25

Doctor: <u>Unless</u> you <u>cut</u> down on salt and fat your health will <u>suffer</u>.

Patient: <u>But</u> it's so <u>difficult</u>! I already <u>run</u> every day for my health.

Doctor: I <u>understand</u>. <u>But</u> good health is the <u>result</u> of both exercise and diet. You <u>must</u> <u>cut</u> down.

CD Three, track 26

medium u /u/ OO

medial	final
include influence introduce produce* reduce rule suit sure**	blue true you

***Note:** There are two pronunciations (and meanings) for this word. Stress on the first syllable is a noun (PRO·duce); stress on the last syllable is a verb (pro·DUCE).

****Note: sure** uses a medium **u** in more careful pronunciation. In relaxed conversation, it may be pronounced /ʃ ɾ/.

And note that the spellings **o** and **ou** in **do** and **you** may also be pronounced with the medium **u** sound.

CD Three, track 27

Student A: Do you have any influence with your boss? I'm looking for work.

Student B: I'm not sure about influence, but I can introduce you.

Student A: Thanks! Any advice about how I might produce the best impression?

Student B: In fact, I do. As a rule, I think it's best to wear a blue or gray suit.

CD Three, track 28

long u /yu/ YOO

initial	medial	final
U.S.	communicate	argue
united	computer	continue
university	contribute	value
use*	f<u>u</u>ture	
used	music	
usually	popular	
	refuse**	

*Note: **use** is pronounced /yuz/ when it's a verb and /yus/ when it's a noun.*

**Note: *There are two pronunciations (and meanings) for this word. Stress on the last syllable is a verb (ref·USE); stress on the first syllable is a noun (REF·use).*

CD Three, track 29

Mother: Which <u>university</u> do you think you'll go to in the <u>future</u>?

Son: For me, a <u>university</u> education has no <u>value</u>. I want to learn rock <u>music</u>.

Mother: I <u>refuse</u> to <u>argue</u> with you. But please <u>continue</u> school until you finish 12th grade!

CD Three, track 30

---

special u pronunciations

silent u	u pronounced as /ʊ/ U	ou pronounced as /ʊ/ U
because brought building buy cause country daughter enough guard	full pull push put sugar	could should would

CD Three, track 31

Student 1: I notice you don't put sugar in your coffee anymore.

Student 2: Yeah. That's because my daughter tells me I should lose weight.

Student 1: Hmm. I could lose a few pounds, too. My problem is I don't buy enough fruits and vegetables.

Student 2: Me neither. All the sugars and fats we eat in this country cause a big obesity problem.

CD Three, track 32

v /v/ V

initial	medial	final
verb	avoid	above
very	even	believe
view	every	drive
visit	however	give
voice	invite	have
vote	never	leave
vowel	over	live
	several	love
	travel	move

CD Three, track 33

Student A: What do you plan to <u>visit</u> when you <u>travel</u> to Victoria?

Student B: Well, I've <u>never</u> been there. <u>However</u>, I <u>believe</u> the Butchart gardens are famous. Also, the <u>view</u> <u>over</u> the harbor is <u>very</u> pretty, I think.

Student A: I'm sure you'll <u>love</u> it! <u>Have</u> a safe <u>drive</u>!

CD Three, track 34

w /w/ W

initial	medial	final
walk	always	below
weather/whether	away	few
well	between	know
what	news	slow
when	own	snow
where		
why		
wish		
with		
worry		
would		

CD Three, track 35

Wife: Please <u>slow</u> down! There's <u>snow</u> on the ground.

Husband: I <u>know</u>! I <u>wish</u> you <u>wouldn't</u> <u>worry</u>. I <u>always</u> drive safely, don't I?

Wife: <u>Well</u>, <u>with</u> this <u>weather</u>, everyone should drive <u>below</u> the speed limit.

CD Three, track 36

silent w

initial	medial	final
who	answer	draw
whole	knowledge	law
whose	toward	saw
wreck	two	
write		
written		
wrong		
wrote		

CD Three, track 37

Student A: My car is <u>wreck</u>ed! Someone turned the <u>wrong</u> way in the parking lot and hit me.

Student B: <u>Who</u> <u>saw</u> the accident?

Student A: The parking lot attendant <u>saw</u> the <u>whole</u> thing. He <u>wrote</u> down his telephone number and said he could <u>draw</u> a picture of what happened.

CD Three, track 38

x /ks/ and /gz/ KS and GZ

medial /ks/ KS	medial /gz/ GZ	final /ks/ KS
excellent	exact	box
except	examine	complex*
exercise	example	fix
expect		mix
expensive		six
experience		tax
explain		
next		

Note: There are two pronunciations (and meanings) for this word. The adjective can be stressed on the first or last syllable (com·PLEX); the noun form is stressed on the first syllable (COM·plex).

CD Three, track 39

Nurse: The doctor will see you next. But before he examines you, we need some information.

Patient: For example?

Nurse: For example, can you explain exactly how you injured your elbow?

Patient: Well, I was exercising at the gym six weeks ago. I experienced a sudden sharp pain. I didn't expect the pain to last so long!

CD Three, track 40

short y /y/ Y

initial	medial	final
year	always	away
yes	eyes	buy
yet		day
you		enjoy
young		may
your		play
yesterday		stay
		they
		way

CD Three, track 41

Student A: Are <u>you</u> planning to go <u>away</u> this <u>year</u> for Christmas?

Student B: We <u>may</u>. We haven't decided <u>yet</u>. How about <u>you</u>?

Student A: <u>Yes</u>. We <u>always</u> <u>stay</u> with the kids. We <u>enjoy</u> <u>play</u>ing with our grandkids.

Student B: It's a special time when <u>they</u> are <u>young</u>, isn't it?

CD Three, track 42

long y /iʸ/ EE

medial	final	
anywhere	actually	hurry
everything	busy	many
	city	money
	country	only
	early	probably
	easy	ready
	family	really
	finally	usually
	happy	very

CD Three, track 43

Student A: We've been in this <u>country</u> for ten years, and we've <u>finally</u> saved enough <u>money</u> for a house.

Student B: <u>Really</u>? Congratulations! When are you and your <u>family</u> moving?

Student A: <u>Actually</u>, we're not in a <u>hurry</u> to go <u>anywhere</u>. We're <u>only</u> looking at houses around the <u>city</u> right now. We'll <u>probably</u> be <u>ready</u> to move <u>early</u> next year.

Student B: Well, good luck with <u>everything</u>. I'm sure you'll be <u>very</u> <u>happy</u> in your own home.

CD Three, track 44

diphthong y /aʸ/ AY

medial	final
myself type	apply buy/by cry dry fly my sky try why

CD Three, track 45

Student A: <u>Why</u> don't you <u>apply</u> for the hostess job at the new coffee shop?

Student B: I don't think that's <u>my type</u> of work. But I might <u>try</u> to get the waitress job.

Student A: Well, let's go <u>by</u> their office together. I might <u>apply</u> for the hostess job <u>myself</u>.

CD Three, track 46

z pronounced /z/ Z and /ts/ TS

initial /z/	medial /z/ and /ts/	final /z/
zero zoo	citizen dozen frozen magazine pizza*	apologize organize prize realize recognize size

***Note:** The **zz** in this, and many other Italian words, is pronounced /ts/.*

CD Three, track 47

Wife: I <u>apologize</u>, but I'm just too tired and too <u>disorganized</u> to prepare dinner tonight.

Husband: No problem. How about I pick up a <u>frozen</u> <u>pizza</u>?

Wife: Fine, but make it two. Large <u>size</u>. Your brother's coming over, and last time he ate at least a <u>dozen</u> slices!

CD Three, track 48

Expansion Activities

Activity 1: Ask Me!

Choose 6 words from today's word list. Use each in a question you'd like to ask a classmate tomorrow:

1. _____

2. _____

3. _____

4. _____

5. _____

6. _____

Activity 2: My Favorite Song

A. Write the name of your favorite English-language song:

_____

B. Listen to the song and find words with the letter and sound from today's lesson. Write them here:

C. Bring the CD and share it with the class, or sing the song yourself!

Activity 3: Cut It Out!

Look in a newspaper, magazine, or flyer for words with the letter and sound from today's lesson. Cut out the words and glue them below:

Activity 4: Picture This!

Bring a favorite picture or photo from home, or draw one yourself. Be ready to talk about the picture with your classmate. Use at least six words with the letter and sound from today's lesson in your description of the picture. Write the words here:

1.

2.

3.

4.

5.

6.

Activity 5: Minimal Pairs

Go to www.ManyThings.org ("Interesting Things for ESL Students"). Under "Speaking," click on "Pronunciation." Choose *Minimal Pairs—Lesson* _____ .

Listen, practice, and take the quiz.

Write the four word pairs below. Be ready to pronounce them in class tomorrow.

_____   _____

_____   _____

_____   _____

_____   _____

Activity 6: Be a Couch Potato!

Watch your favorite TV program. Listen for words with the letter and sound from today's lesson. Write them below.

Name of TV program: _____

Words:

_____   _____

_____   _____

_____   _____

_____   _____

_____   _____

_____   _____

Activity 7: It's All About Me

Choose 6 words from today's word list. Use each in a true sentence about yourself. Then read the sentences to a classmate:

1._____

2. _____

3. _____

4._____

5. _____

6. _____

Activity 8: What's New?

Go to www.voanews/learningenglish/home.

Choose one news story (listening or captioned video).

Write the title: _____

Write 6 words from the news story that have the letter and sound from today's lesson. Discuss the news story with a classmate tomorrow, using the 6 words:

1. _____

2. _____

3. _____

4. _____

5. _____

6. _____

Activity 9: Food for Thought

Look at the packages of food in your kitchen. How many foods or brand names have the letter and sound from today's lesson? Write them here:

1. _____

2. _____

3. _____

4. _____

5. _____

6. _____

7. _____

8. _____

9. _____

10. _____

Activity 10: Hit the Road!

Read the street signs in the neighborhood of your school or home (or look at a map). How many street names have the letter and sound from today's lesson? Write them here:

1. _____

2. _____

3. _____

4. _____

5. _____

6. _____

7. _____

8. _____

9. _____

10. _____

Contrasting Pairs

Procedure:

Each of the following pages has four activities working with contrasting pairs. If you are using the CDs, use the pause button after Activity 1. Activity 2 does not use the CD. After doing it, release the pause button to continue on to Activities 3 and 4.

If you are not using the CDs, the words in the boxes may be read to the students in three different patterns. One pattern is to read all the words with the same sound first, for example: *each, eat, ease,* etc. Then all the words with the other sound: *itch, is, it,* etc. The second alternative pattern would be to read the contrasting pairs: *each – itch, eat – it,* etc. A third alternative is to read both patterns: first *each, eat,* etc., and then *each – it,* etc. Then, as in Activity 2, read one of the paired words and have the students raise their fingers to indicate which they hear.

Pairs:

/iʸ/ **EE seat** - /I/ **I sit**   84

/eʸ/ **AI late** - /ɛ/ **E let**   85

/ɛ/ **E end** - /æ/ **A and**   86

/æ/ **A an** - /a/ **AH on**   87

/ə/ **UH shut** - /uʷ/ **OO shoot**   88

/ə/ **UH once** - /a/ **AH wants**   89

/r̩/ **ER work** - /a/ **AH walk**   90

/oʷ/ **O own** - /a/ **AH on**   91

/æʷ/ **OU now** - /oʷ/ **O know**   92

/p/ **P pig** - /b/ **B big**   93

Contrasting Pairs 1

/iʸ/ EE *seat* /I/ I *sit*

Activity 1: Listen and repeat each pair of words:

1. each – itch	6. read – rid
2. eat – it	7. seat – sit
3. ease – is	8. seeks – six
4. feel – fill	9. we'll - will
5. green - grin	

Activity 2: Your partner will choose one word at random from each pair to pronounce. If you hear the first word (each), raise one finger ☝. If you hear the second word (itch), raise two fingers ✌. Discuss any mistakes. Reverse roles.

Activity 3: Listen and repeat each *Phrase 1* and *Phrase 2*. Example:
What does "each" mean?   Every.

Phrase 1	*Phrase 2*
1. What does "**each**" mean?	Every.
What does "**itch**" mean?	To want to scratch.
2. The mother said, "**Eat**...	your lunch."
The mother said, "**It**...	isn't bedtime."
3. Can you **feel**...	the warm sun?
Can you **fill**...	this bowl with apples?
4. James said, "**We'll**...	sit together."
James said, "**Will**...	you come tomorrow?"

Activity 4: Listen and respond: You will hear the first or second *Phrase 1*. Say the correct *Phrase 2*. (Independent learners check your answers with the Answer Key.)

Activity 5: Your partner will choose the first or second *Phrase 1* from each pair and say it. Say the correct *Phrase 2*. Discuss any mistakes. Reverse roles.

Answers page 108
Contrasting Pairs CD One, track 1

Contrasting Pairs 2

/eʸ/ **AI** *late* - /ɛ/ **E** *let*

Activity 1: Listen and repeat each pair of words:

1. aid - Ed	5. main - men
2. baste - best	6. raid - read
3. gate - get	7. wait - wet
4. late - let	8. whale - well

Activity 2: Your partner will choose one word at random from each pair to pronounce. If you hear the first word (late), raise one finger ☝. If you hear the second word (let), raise two fingers ✌. Discuss any mistakes. Reverse roles.

Activity 3: Listen and repeat each *Phrase 1* and *Phrase 2*. Example:
*Get **aid** right away.*   *We need help.*

Phrase 1	*Phrase 2*
1. Get **aid** right away.	We need help.
Get **Ed** right away.	We want him.
2. What does "**late**" mean?	The opposite of "early."
What does "**let**" mean?	Allow or permit.
3. Did you find the **main**…	entrance?
Did you find the **men**…	and women?
4. Please **wait**…	for me here.
Please **wet**…	the dog's fur.

Activity 4: Listen and respond: You will hear the first or second *Phrase 1*. Say the correct *Phrase 2*. (Independent learners check your answers with the Answer Key.)

Activity 5: Your partner will choose the first or second *Phrase 1* from each pair and say it. Say the correct *Phrase 2*. Discuss any mistakes. Reverse roles.

Answers page 108
Contrasting Pairs CD One, track 2

Contrasting Pairs 3

/ɛ/ E *end* – /æ/ A *and*

Activity 1: Listen and repeat each pair of words:

1. bed - bad	5. left - laughed
2. Em - am	6. men - man
3. end - and	7. wren - ran
4. head - had	

Activity 2: Your partner will choose one word at random from each pair to pronounce. If you hear the first word (end), raise one finger ☝. If you hear the second word (and), raise two fingers ✌. Discuss any mistakes. Reverse roles.

Activity 3: Listen and repeat each *Phrase 1* and *Phrase 2*. Example:
There was a **bed**...   in the room.

Phrase 1	*Phrase 2*
1. There was a **bed**...	in the room.
There was a **bad**...	accident.
2. He **left** when she told the joke.	He didn't like it.
He **laughed** when she told the joke.	He thought it was funny.
3. I saw the **men**.	There were 25.
I saw the **man**.	He was alone.
4. Did you say "**wren**"?	Yes. A small bird.
Did you say "**ran**"?	Yes. The past of "run."

Activity 4: Listen and respond: You will hear the first or second *Phrase 1*. Say the correct *Phrase 2*. (Independent learners check your answers with the Answer Key.)

Activity 5: Your partner will choose the first or second *Phrase 1* from each pair and say it. Say the correct *Phrase 2*. Discuss any mistakes. Reverse roles.

Answers page 108
Contrasting Pairs CD One, track 3

Contrasting Pairs 4

/æ/ A *an* − /a/ AH *on*

Activity 1: Listen and repeat each pair of words:

1. Al - all	6. gnat - not
2. an - on	7. jab - job
3. at - ought	8. ran - Ron
4. bat - bought	9. rang - wrong
5. glass - gloss	10. tack - talk

Activity 2: Your partner will choose one word at random from each pair to pronounce. If you hear the first word (an), raise one finger ☝. If you hear the second word (on), raise two fingers ✌. Discuss any mistakes. Reverse roles.

Activity 3: Listen and repeat each *Phrase 1* and *Phrase 2*. Example:
Give **Al** the money…   for the rent.

Phrase 1	*Phrase 2*
1. Give **Al** the money…	for the rent.
Give **all** the money…	to the poor people.
2. Those players **bat**…	instead of pitch.
Those players **bought**…	new uniforms.
3. He gave me a **jab**…	with his finger.
He gave me a **job**…	for $15 an hour.
4. Please **tack**…	the paper on the wall.
Please **talk**…	to me.

Activity 4: Listen and respond: You will hear the first or second *Phrase 1*. Say the correct *Phrase 2*. (Independent learners check your answers with the Answer Key.)

Activity 5: Your partner will choose the first or second *Phrase 1* from each pair and say it. Say the correct *Phrase 2*. Discuss any mistakes. Reverse roles.

Answers page 108
Contrasting Pairs CD One, track 4

Contrasting Pairs 5

/ə/ UH *shut* – /uʷ/ OO *shoot*

Activity 1: Listen and repeat each pair of words:

> 1. but - boot
> 2. cut - coot
> 3. just - juiced
> 4. shut - shoot

Activity 2: Your partner will choose one word at random from each pair to pronounce. If you hear the first word (shut), raise one finger ☝. If you hear the second word (shoot), raise two fingers ✌. Discuss any mistakes. Reverse roles.

Activity 3: Listen and repeat each *Phrase 1* and *Phrase 2*. Example:
*How do you spell "**but**"?   B-U-T.*

Phrase 1	Phrase 2
1. How do you spell "**but**"?	B-U-T.
How do you spell "**boot**"?	B-O-O-T.
2. What does "**cut**" mean?	To slice with a knife.
What does "**coot**" mean?	A water bird.
3. She **just**...	woke up.
She **juiced**...	the oranges.
4. Don't **shut**...	that window.
Don't **shoot**...	that gun.

Activity 4: Listen and respond: You will hear the first or second *Phrase 1*. Say the correct *Phrase 2*. (Independent learners check your answers with the Answer Key.)

Activity 5: Your partner will choose the first or second *Phrase 1* from each pair and say it. Say the correct *Phrase 2*. Discuss any mistakes. Reverse roles.

Answers page 108
Contrasting Pairs CD One, track 5

Contrasting Pairs 6

/ə/ UH *once* – /a/ AH *wants*

Activity 1: Listen and repeat each pair of words:

1. but - bought	5. done - Don
2. color - collar	6. once - wants
3. come - calm	7. run - Ron
4. cut - caught	8. shut - shot

Activity 2: Your partner will choose one word at random from each pair to pronounce. If you hear the first word (once), raise one finger ✌. If you hear the second word (wants), raise two fingers ✌. Discuss any mistakes. Reverse roles.

Activity 3: Listen and repeat each *Phrase 1* and *Phrase 2*. Example:
*I don't like that **color**.*   *I prefer blue.*

Phrase 1	*Phrase 2*
1. I don't like that **color**.	I prefer blue.
I don't like that **collar**.	I want a t-shirt.
2. Please **come** down.	I'm on the first floor.
Please **calm** down.	Relax!
3. Toshi **cut** the fish...	into sushi slices.
Toshi **caught** the fish...	at the lake.
4. The soldier **shut** the door...	when he left.
The soldier **shot** the door...	with his gun.

Activity 4: Listen and respond: You will hear the first or second *Phrase 1*. Say the correct *Phrase 2*. (Independent learners check your answers with the Answer Key.)

Activity 5: Your partner will choose the first or second *Phrase 1* from each pair and say it. Say the correct *Phrase 2.* Discuss any mistakes. Reverse roles.

Answers page 108
Contrasting Pairs CD One, track 6

Contrasting Pairs 7

/ṛ/ ER *work* – /a/ AH *walk*

Activity 1: Listen and repeat each pair of words:

> 1. earn - on
> 2. girl - gall
> 3. learn - lawn
> 4. word - wad
> 5. work - walk

Activity 2: Your partner will choose one word at random from each pair to pronounce. If you hear the first word (work), raise one finger ☝. If you hear the second word (walk), raise two fingers ✌. Discuss any mistakes. Reverse roles.

Activity 3: Listen and repeat each *Phrase 1* and *Phrase 2*. Example:
*How do you spell "**earn**"?*   *E-A-R-N.*

Phrase 1	*Phrase 2*
1. How do you spell "**earn**"?	E-A-R-N.
How do you spell "**on**"?	O-N.
2. He's having problems with his **girl**-	friend.
He's having problems with his **gall**	bladder.
3. That big **word**…	is hard to pronounce.
That big **wad**…	of money is not mine.
4. On weekdays, I always **work**…	at my office.
On weekdays, I always **walk**…	to school.

Activity 4: Listen and respond: You will hear the first or second *Phrase 1*. Say the correct *Phrase 2*. (Independent learners check your answers with the Answer Key.)

Activity 5: Your partner will choose the first or second *Phrase 1* from each pair and say it. Say the correct *Phrase 2*. Discuss any mistakes. Reverse roles.

Answers page 108
Contrasting Pairs CD One, track 7

Contrasting Pairs 8

/oʷ/ O *own* – /a/ AH *on*

Activity 1: Listen and repeat each pair of words:

> 1. boat - bought
> 2. coast - cost
> 3. goat - got
> 4. note - not
> 5. own - on

Activity 2: Your partner will choose one word at random from each pair to pronounce. If you hear the first word (own), raise one finger ☝. If you hear the second word (on), raise two fingers ✌. Discuss any mistakes. Reverse roles.

Activity 3: Listen and repeat each *Phrase 1* and *Phrase 2*. Example:
What does "boat" mean?   *A small ship.*

Phrase 1	*Phrase 2*
1. What does "**boat**" mean? What does "**bought**" mean?	A small ship. The past of "buy."
2. The country's **coast**… The country's **cost**…	is on the Pacific Ocean. of living is high.
3. We will **note**… We will **not**…	the address and telephone. be late.
4. How do you spell "**own**"? How do you spell "**on**"?	O-W-N. O-N.

Activity 4: Listen and respond: You will hear the first or second *Phrase 1*. Say the correct *Phrase 2*. (Independent learners check your answers with the Answer Key.)

Activity 5: Your partner will choose the first or second *Phrase 1* from each pair and say it. Say the correct *Phrase 2*. Discuss any mistakes. Reverse roles.

Answers page 108
Contrasting Pairs CD One, track 8

Contrasting Pairs 9

/æʷ/ OU *now* – /oʷ/ O *know*

Activity 1: Listen and repeat each pair of words:

1. about – a boat	5. now - know
2. how - hoe	6. out - oat
3. loud - load	7. ow - owe
4. noun - known	8. town - tone

Activity 2: Your partner will choose one word at random from each pair to pronounce. If you hear the first word (now), raise one finger ☝. If you hear the second word (know), raise two fingers ✌. Discuss any mistakes. Reverse roles.

Activity 3: Listen and repeat each *Phrase 1* and *Phrase 2*. Example:
I'll rent **about**…   100 chairs for the party.

Phrase 1	*Phrase 2*
1. I'll rent **about**…	100 chairs for the party.
I'll rent **a boat**…	to sail on the lake.
2. That was a **loud**…	noise.
That was a **load**…	of rocks for the garden.
3. What does "**out**" mean?	The opposite of "in."
What does "**oat**" mean?	A kind of grain.
4. I love that **town**.	It's where I was born.
I love that **tone**.	It's a beautiful sound.

Activity 4: Listen and respond: You will hear the first or second *Phrase 1*. Say the correct *Phrase 2*. (Independent learners check your answers with the Answer Key.)

Activity 5: Your partner will choose the first or second *Phrase 1* from each pair and say it. Say the correct *Phrase 2*. Discuss any mistakes. Reverse roles.

Answers page 108
Contrasting Pairs CD One, track 9

Contrasting Pairs 10

/p/ P pig – /b/ B *big*

Activity 1: Listen and repeat each pair of words:

1. appear - a beer	5. poor - bore
2. pack - back	6. pull - bull
3. path - bath	7. push - bush
4. pig - big	

Activity 2: Your partner will choose one word at random from each pair to pronounce. If you hear the first word (pig), raise one finger ☝. If you hear the second word (big), raise two fingers ✌. Discuss any mistakes. Reverse roles.

Activity 3: Listen and repeat each *Phrase 1* and *Phrase 2*. Example:
*Please use the **pack**...*   of playing cards..

Phrase 1	*Phrase 2*
1. Please use the **pack**...	of playing cards.
Please use the **back**...	door.
2. She's taking a long **path**.	Yes, it's 2 miles.
She's taking a long **bath**.	Yes, for an hour.
3. That teacher's a **poor**...	man. He's not rich.
That teacher's a **bore**.	He's not interesting.
4. Give him a **push**...	into the swimming pool.
Give him a **bush**...	for the garden.

Activity 4: Listen and respond: You will hear the first or second *Phrase 1*. Say the correct *Phrase 2*. (Independent learners check your answers with the Answer Key.)

Activity 5: Your partner will choose the first or second *Phrase 1* from each pair and say it. Say the correct *Phrase 2*. Discuss any mistakes. Reverse roles.

Answers page 108
Contrasting Pairs CD One, track 10

Contrasting Pairs 11

/p/ P *past* – /f/ F *fast*

Activity 1: Listen and repeat each pair of words:

1. past - fast	5. pour - for
2. peel - feel	6. pull - full
3. pill - fill	7. put - foot
4. pine - fine	

Activity 2: Your partner will choose one word at random from each pair to pronounce. If you hear the first word (past), raise one finger ☝. If you hear the second word (fast), raise two fingers ✌. Discuss any mistakes. Reverse roles.

Activity 3: Listen and repeat each *Phrase 1* and *Phrase 2*. Example:
*The car went **past**…*   *me. It didn't stop.*

Phrase 1	*Phrase 2*
1. The car went **past**…	me. It didn't stop.
The car went **fast**.	It was speeding.
2. Please **peel** the apple.	Take off the skin.
Please **feel** the apple.	Is it hard or soft?
3. That tree is **pine**.	It's for Christmas.
That tree is **fine**.	I like it.
4. The sign says, "**Pull**,…	Don't Push."
The sign says, "**Full**,…	Park on the Next Level."

Activity 4: Listen and respond: You will hear the first or second *Phrase 1*. Say the correct *Phrase 2*. (Independent learners check your answers with the Answer Key.)

Activity 5: Your partner will choose the first or second *Phrase 1* from each pair and say it. Say the correct *Phrase 2*. Discuss any mistakes. Reverse roles.

Answers page 108
Contrasting Pairs CD One, track 11

Contrasting Pairs 12

/t/ **T** *time* — /d/ **D** *dime*

Activity 1: Listen and repeat each pair of words:

1. time - dime	4. at - ad
2. to - do	5. great - grade
3. town - down	6. hat - had
	7. let - led
	8. mate - made
	9. neat - need
	10. set - said

Activity 2: Your partner will choose one word at random from each pair to pronounce. If you hear the first word (time), raise one finger ☝. If you hear the second word (dime), raise two fingers ✌. Discuss any mistakes. Reverse roles.

Activity 3: Listen and repeat each *Phrase 1* and *Phrase 2*. Example:
Do you have the **time***?*   *Yes. It's 5 o'clock.*

Phrase 1	*Phrase 2*
1. Do you have the **time**?	Yes. It's 5 o'clock.
Do you have the **dime**?	No. I spent it.
2. What is "**town**"?	A small city.
What is "**down**"?	The opposite of "up."
3. The mother **let** the child...	eat candy.
The mother **led** the child...	to the bathroom.
4. He **set** his wallet...	on the table.
He **said**, "His wallet...	has no money inside."

Activity 4: Listen and respond: You will hear the first or second *Phrase 1*. Say the correct *Phrase 2*. (Independent learners check your answers with the Answer Key.)

Activity 5: Your partner will choose the first or second *Phrase 1* from each pair and say it. Say the correct *Phrase 2*. Discuss any mistakes. Reverse roles.

Answers page 108
Contrasting Pairs CD One, track 12

Contrasting Pairs 13

/v/ V *very* — /b/ B *berry*

Activity 1: Listen and repeat each pair of words:

> 1. V - B
> 2. van - ban
> 3. very - berry
> 4. vote - boat

Activity 2: Your partner will choose one word at random from each pair to pronounce. If you hear the first word (very), raise one finger ☝. If you hear the second word (berry), raise two fingers ✌. Discuss any mistakes. Reverse roles.

Activity 3: Listen and repeat each *Phrase 1* and *Phrase 2*. Example:
> *Use the letter **V** to spell...*   *"love."*

Phrase 1	*Phrase 2*
1. Use the letter **V** to spell...	"love."
Use the letter **B** to spell...	"boy."
2. There is a **van**...	in the parking lot.
There is a **ban**...	on smoking in restaurants.
3. That's **very**...	interesting.
That's **berry**...	pie.
4. Let's take a **vote**...	to choose the president.
Let's take a **boat**...	to the island.

Activity 4: Listen and respond: You will hear the first or second *Phrase 1*. Say the correct *Phrase 2*. (Independent learners check your answers with the Answer Key.)

Activity 5: Your partner will choose the first or second *Phrase 1* from each pair and say it. Say the correct *Phrase 2*. Discuss any mistakes. Reverse roles.

Answers page 109
Contrasting Pairs CD Two, track 1

Contrasting Pairs 14

/θ/ **th** *through* — /t/ **T** *true*

Activity 1: Listen and repeat each pair of words:

> 1. thanks - tanks
> 2. thought - taught
> 3. through - true
> 4. both - boat

Activity 2: Your partner will choose one word at random from each pair to pronounce. If you hear the first word (through), raise one finger ☝. If you hear the second word (true), raise two fingers ✌. Discuss any mistakes. Reverse roles.

Activity 3: Listen and repeat each *Phrase 1* and *Phrase 2*. Example:
*Mark said, "**Thanks**...   for the gift."*

Phrase 1	*Phrase 2*
1. Mark said, "**Thanks**...	for the gift."
Mark said, "**Tanks**...	destroyed the city."
2. She **thought** English...	was easier than Spanish.
She **taught** English...	in college.
3. You and I are **through**.	I don't love you anymore.
You and I are **true**...	friends.
4. John gave her **both**...	a necklace and a ring.
John gave her **boat**...	a good cleaning.

Activity 4: Listen and respond: You will hear the first or second *Phrase 1*. Say the correct *Phrase 2*. (Independent learners check your answers with the Answer Key.)

Activity 5: Your partner will choose the first or second *Phrase 1* from each pair and say it. Say the correct *Phrase 2*. Discuss any mistakes. Reverse roles.

Answers page 109
Contrasting Pairs CD Two, track 2

Contrasting Pairs 15

/ð/ **TH** *they* – /d/ **D** *day*

Activity 1: Listen and repeat each pair of words:

> 1. than - Dan
> 2. then - den
> 3. they - day
> 4. though - dough
> 5. breathe - breed

Activity 2: Your partner will choose one word at random from each pair to pronounce. If you hear the first word (they), raise one finger ☝. If you hear the second word (day), raise two fingers ✌. Discuss any mistakes. Reverse roles.

Activity 3: Listen and repeat each *Phrase 1* and *Phrase 2*. Example:
    *When will **they** come?*   *For dinner at 6:00.*

Phrase 1	*Phrase 2*
1. When will **they** come?	For dinner at 6:00.
When will **day** come?	After the night.
2. What does "**then**" mean?	Next.
What does "**den**" mean?	A lion's home.
3. "**Though**" is used…	to connect sentences.
Dough is used…	to make bread.
4. Mr. and Mrs. Jones **breathe**…	the fresh country air.
Mr. and Mrs. Jones **breed**…	expensive dogs.

Activity 4: Listen and respond: You will hear the first or second *Phrase 1*. Say the correct *Phrase 2*. (Independent learners check your answers with the Answer Key.)

Activity 5: Your partner will choose the first or second *Phrase 1* from each pair and say it. Say the correct *Phrase 2*. Discuss any mistakes. Reverse roles.

Answers page 109
Contrasting Pairs CD Two, track 3

Contrasting Pairs 16

/s/ S *ice* – /z/ Z *eyes*

Activity 1: Listen and repeat each pair of words:

1. dance - Dan's	5. Miss - Ms.
2. face - faze	6. once - one's
3. ice - eyes	7. race - raise
4. loose - lose	8. see - Z

Activity 2: Your partner will choose one word at random from each pair to pronounce. If you hear the first word (ice), raise one finger ☝. If you hear the second word (eyes), raise two fingers ✌. Discuss any mistakes. Reverse roles.

Activity 3: Listen and repeat each *Phrase 1* and *Phrase 2*. Example:
  I like ice...   in my drinks.

Phrase 1	*Phrase 2*
1. I like **ice**...	in my drinks.
I like **eyes**...	that are green.
2. The opposite of "**loose**"...	is "tight."
The opposite of "**lose**"...	is "win."
3. Who's that with **Miss** Brown?	Her fiancé.
Who's that with **Ms.** Brown?	Her husband.
4. Did she **race** the children?	Yes, but they ran faster.
Did she **raise** the children?	Yes. She's their mother.

Activity 4: Listen and respond: You will hear the first or second *Phrase 1*. Say the correct *Phrase 2*. (Independent learners check your answers with the Answer Key.)

Activity 5: Your partner will choose the first or second *Phrase 1* from each pair and say it. Say the correct *Phrase 2*. Discuss any mistakes. Reverse roles.

Answers page 109
Contrasting Pairs CD Two, track 4

Contrasting Pairs 17

/S/ S *see* – /ʃ/ SH *she*

Activity 1: Listen and repeat each pair of words:

> 1. said - shed
> 2. saw - Shaw
> 3. see - she
> 4. so - show
> 5. Sue's - shoes

Activity 2: Your partner will choose one word at random from each pair to pronounce. If you hear the first word (see), raise one finger ☝. If you hear the second word (she), raise two fingers ✌. Discuss any mistakes. Reverse roles.

Activity 3: Listen and repeat each *Phrase 1* and *Phrase 2*. Example:
*What does "**said**" mean?*   *The past of "say."*

Phrase 1	Phrase 2
1. What does "**said**" mean?	The past of "say."
What does "**shed**" mean?	A building for garden tools.
2. "**See**," "saw…"	and "seen" are verbs.
She saw…	my new car.
3. This closet is for **Sue's**…	coat.
This closet is for **shoes**…	and boots.
4. The man said, "**So**…	long!"
The man said, "**Show**…	me your I.D."

Activity 4: Listen and respond: You will hear the first or second *Phrase 1*. Say the correct *Phrase 2*. (Independent learners check your answers with the Answer Key.)

Activity 5: Your partner will choose the first or second *Phrase 1* from each pair and say it. Say the correct *Phrase 2*. Discuss any mistakes. Reverse roles.

Answers page 109
Contrasting Pairs CD Two, track 5

Contrasting Pairs 18

/h/ H *hate* – "dropped h" *eight*

Activity 1: Listen and repeat each pair of words:

1. had - ad	5. head - Ed
2. has - as	6. here - ear
3. hate - eight	7. his - is
4. he - E	8. how - ow

Activity 2: Your partner will choose one word at random from each pair to pronounce. If you hear the first word (hate), raise one finger ☝. If you hear the second word (eight), raise two fingers ✌. Discuss any mistakes. Reverse roles.

Activity 3: Listen and repeat each *Phrase 1* and *Phrase 2*. Example:
   Is **hate**…   necessary?

Phrase 1	*Phrase 2*
1. Is **hate**…	necessary?
Is **eight**…	enough?
2. **He** comes before…	6:00 in the morning.
E comes before…	F in the alphabet.
3. Julie said, "**Head**…	towards the mountains."
Julie said, "**Ed**…	is my cousin."
4. **His** English…	is fluent.
Is English…	difficult?

Activity 4: Listen and respond: You will hear the first or second *Phrase 1*. Say the correct *Phrase 2*. (Independent learners check your answers with the Answer Key.)

Activity 5: Your partner will choose the first or second *Phrase 1* from each pair and say it. Say the correct *Phrase 2*. Discuss any mistakes. Reverse roles.

Answers page 109
Contrasting Pairs CD Two, track 6

Contrasting Pairs 19

/n/ N *no* – /l/ L *low*

Activity 1: Listen and repeat each pair of words:

1. need - lead	5. mean - meal
2. no - low	6. ten - tell
3. fine - file	7. when - well
4. in - ill	

Activity 2: Your partner will choose one word at random from each pair to pronounce. If you hear the first word (no), raise one finger ☝. If you hear the second word (low), raise two fingers ✌. Discuss any mistakes. Reverse roles.

Activity 3: Listen and repeat each *Phrase 1* and *Phrase 2*. Example:
*Did you **need** the horses…   to pull the cart?*

Phrase 1	Phrase 2
1. Did you **need** the horses…	to pull the cart?
Did you **lead** the horses…	to the barn?
2. There are **no** chairs.	Please get some.
There are **low** chairs…	for the small children.
3. The **fine**…	for speeding was $300.
The **file**…	was in the cabinet.
4. She was **in**…	school to learn English.
She was **ill**…	with the flu.

Activity 4: Listen and respond: You will hear the first or second *Phrase 1*. Say the correct *Phrase 2*. (Independent learners check your answers with the Answer Key.)

Activity 5: Your partner will choose the first or second *Phrase 1* from each pair and say it. Say the correct *Phrase 2*. Discuss any mistakes. Reverse roles.

Answers page 109
Contrasting Pairs CD Two, track 7

Contrasting Pairs 20

/n/ N *thin* – /ŋ/ NG *thing*

Activity 1: Listen and repeat each pair of words:

> 1. a lawn - along
> 2. done - dung
> 3. lawn - long
> 4. sin - sing
> 5. thin - thing

Activity 2: Your partner will choose one word at random from each pair to pronounce. If you hear the first word (thin), raise one finger ☝. If you hear the second word (thing), raise two fingers ✌. Discuss any mistakes. Reverse roles.

Activity 3: Listen and repeat each *Phrase 1* and *Phrase 2*. Example:
> *Did you get **a lawn**...*   *and a garden with your condo?*

Phrase 1	*Phrase 2*
1. Did you get **a lawn**... Did you get **along**...	and a garden with your condo? with your mother-in-law?
2. What does "**done**" mean? What does "**dung**" mean?	The past participle of "do." Animal waste.
3. James likes to **sin**. James likes to **sing**.	That's terrible! That's great!
4. That **thin**... That **thing**...	man is my son. is a can opener.

Activity 4: Listen and respond: You will hear the first or second *Phrase 1*. Say the correct *Phrase 2*. (Independent learners check your answers with the Answer Key.)

Activity 5: Your partner will choose the first or second *Phrase 1* from each pair and say it. Say the correct *Phrase 2*. Discuss any mistakes. Reverse roles.

Answers page 109
Contrasting Pairs CD Two, track 8

Contrasting Pairs 21

final /n/ N *sun* — final /m/ M *some*

Activity 1: Listen and repeat each pair of words:

> 1. an - am
> 2. done - dumb
> 3. sun - some
> 4. then - them
> 5. warn - warm

Activity 2: Your partner will choose one word at random from each pair to pronounce. If you hear the first word (sun), raise one finger ☝. If you hear the second word (some), raise two fingers ✌. Discuss any mistakes. Reverse roles.

Activity 3: Listen and repeat each *Phrase 1* and *Phrase 2*. Example:
*Julie asked, "**An**...   orange or an apple?"*

Phrase 1	*Phrase 2*
1. Julie asked, "**An**...	orange or an apple?"
Julie asked, "**Am**...	I late?"
2. This job is **done**!	I'm finished!
This job is **dumb**!	It's stupid!
3. There's **sun**-	shine.
There's **some**...	coffee.
4. Did he **warn** you?	Yes, he said, "Be careful!"
Did he **warm** you?	Yes, with a blanket.

Activity 4: Listen and respond: You will hear the first or second *Phrase 1*. Say the correct *Phrase 2*. (Independent learners check your answers with the Answer Key.)

Activity 5: Your partner will choose the first or second *Phrase 1* from each pair and say it. Say the correct *Phrase 2*. Discuss any mistakes. Reverse roles.

Answers page 109
Contrasting Pairs CD Two, track 9

Contrasting Pairs 22

/l/ L *light* – /r/ R *right*

Activity 1: Listen and repeat each pair of words:

1. light - right	5. flee - free
2. alive - arrive	6. little - litter
3. all - are	7. steal - steer
4. call - car	8. tell - tear

Activity 2: Your partner will choose one word at random from each pair to pronounce. If you hear the first word (light), raise one finger ☝. If you hear the second word (right), raise two fingers ✌. Discuss any mistakes. Reverse roles.

Activity 3: Listen and repeat each *Phrase 1* and *Phrase 2*. Example:
   *I wore the **light** shirt.*   *Not the dark one.*

Phrase 1	*Phrase 2*
1. I wore the **light** shirt.	Not the dark one.
I wore the **right** shirt.	Not the wrong one.
2. Will you take my **call**?	I need to talk to you.
Will you take my **car**?	You can drive it.
3. Put the **little**…	sweater on the puppy.
Put the **litter**…	in the trash can.
4. Did you **steal** the car?	No, a thief took it.
Did you **steer** the car?	Yes, I drove it.

Activity 4: Listen and respond: You will hear the first or second *Phrase 1*. Say the correct *Phrase 2*. (Independent learners check your answers with the Answer Key.)

Activity 5: Your partner will choose the first or second *Phrase 1* from each pair and say it. Say the correct *Phrase 2*. Discuss any mistakes. Reverse roles.

Answers page 109
Contrasting Pairs CD Two, track 10

Contrasting Pairs 23

/y/ Y *yet* – /dʒ/ J *jet*

Activity 1: Listen and repeat each pair of words:

> 1. Yale - jail
> 2. yes - Jess
> 3. yet - jet
> 4. yoke - joke

Activity 2: Your partner will choose one word at random from each pair to pronounce. If you hear the first word (yet), raise one finger ☝. If you hear the second word (jet), raise two fingers ✌. Discuss any mistakes. Reverse roles.

Activity 3: Listen and repeat each *Phrase 1* and *Phrase 2*. Example:
> *My son is going to* **Yale**.   *Congratulations!*

Phrase 1	*Phrase 2*
1. My son is going to **Yale**.	Congratulations!
My son is going to **jail**.	That's too bad!
2. The father said, "**Yes**...	I have a son."
The father said, "**Jess**...	is my daughter."
3. How do you spell "**yet**"?	With a "Y."
How do you spell "**jet**"?	With a "J."
4. I don't like the **yolk**.	I only eat egg whites.
I don't like the **joke**.	It's not funny.

Activity 4: Listen and respond: You will hear the first or second *Phrase 1*. Say the correct *Phrase 2*. (Independent learners check your answers with the Answer Key.)

Activity 5: Your partner will choose the first or second *Phrase 1* from each pair and say it. Say the correct *Phrase 2*. Discuss any mistakes. Reverse roles.

Answers page 109
Contrasting Pairs CD Two, track 11

Contrasting Pairs 24

/tʃ/ CH *chair* – **/ʃ/ SH** *share*

Activity 1: Listen and repeat each pair of words:

> 1. chair - share
> 2. chew - shoe
> 3. watch - wash
> 4. which - wish

Activity 2: Your partner will choose one word at random from each pair to pronounce. If you hear the first word (chair), raise one finger ☝. If you hear the second word (share), raise two fingers ✌. Discuss any mistakes. Reverse roles.

Activity 3: Listen and repeat each *Phrase 1* and *Phrase 2*. Example:
> *I don't want a big **chair**...*   *to sit on.*

Phrase 1

1. I don't want a big **chair**...
   I don't want a big **share**...

2. Did you say "**chew**"?
   Did you say "**shoe**"?

3. Please **watch** my car.
   Please **wash** my car.

4. She said, "**Which**...
   She said, "**Wish**...

Phrase 2

to sit on.
of the business profits.

Yes. Eat your food.
Yes. It's in the closet.

Don't let anyone steal it.
It's dirty.

one is mine?"
for world peace."

Activity 4: Listen and respond: You will hear the first or second *Phrase 1*. Say the correct *Phrase 2*. (Independent learners check your answers with the Answer Key.)

Activity 5: Your partner will choose the first or second *Phrase 1* from each pair and say it. Say the correct *Phrase 2*. Discuss any mistakes. Reverse roles.

Answers page 109
Contrasting Pairs CD Two, track 12

ANSWER KEY to Activity 4

Contrasting Pairs 1 – page 84

1. Every
2. your lunch."
3. this bowl with apples?
4. you come tomorrow?"

Contrasting Pairs 2 – page 85

1. We want him.
2. The opposite of "early."
3. and women?
4. for me here.

Contrasting Pairs 3 – page 86

1. accident.
2. He thought it was funny.
3. There were 25.
4. Yes. A small bird.

Contrasting Pairs 4 – page 87

1. for the rent.
2. new uniforms.
3. with his finger.
4. to me.

Contrasting Pairs 5 – page 88

1. B-O-O-T.
2. A water bird.
3. woke up.
4. that window.

Contrasting Pairs 6 – page 89

1. I want a t-shirt.
2. Relax!
3. into sushi slices.
4. when he left.

Contrasting Pairs 7 – page 90

1. O-N.
2. friend.
3. is hard to pronounce.
4. to school.

Contrasting Pairs 8 – page 91

1. A small ship.
2. of living is high.
3. the address and telephone.
4. O-N.

Contrasting Pairs 9 – page 92

1. to sail on the lake.
2. noise.
3. A kind of grain.
4. It's a beautiful sound.

Contrasting Pairs 10 – page 93

1. door.
2. Yes, it's 2 miles.
3. He's not interesting.
4. into the swimming pool.

Contrasting Pairs 11 – page 94

1. me. It didn't stop.
2. Is it hard or soft?
3. I like it.
4. Don't Push."

Contrasting Pairs 12 – page 95

1. No. I spent it.
2. The opposite of "up."
3. eat candy.
4. on the table.

ANSWER KEY to Activity 4

Contrasting Pairs 13 – page 96

1. "boy."
2. in the parking lot.
3. interesting.
4. to the island.

Contrasting Pairs 14 – page 97

1. destroyed the city."
2. was easier than Spanish.
3. friends.
4. a necklace and a ring.

Contrasting Pairs 15 – page 98

1. For dinner at 6:00.
2. A lion's home.
3. to connect sentences.
4. expensive dogs.

Contrasting Pairs 16 – page 99

1. that are green.
2. is "win."
3. Her fiancé.
4. Yes, but they ran faster.

Contrasting Pairs 17 – page 100

1. The past of "say."
2. my new car.
3. coat.
4. me your I.D."

Contrasting Pairs 18 – page 101

1. enough?
2. 6:00 in the morning.
3. is my cousin."
4. is fluent.

Contrasting Pairs 19 – page 102

1. to the barn?
2. for the small children.
3. for speeding was $300.
4. school to learn English.

Contrasting Pairs 20 – page 103

1. and a garden with your condo?
2. Animal waste.
3. That's terrible!
4. is a can opener.

Contrasting Pairs 21 – page 104

1. I late?"
2. It's stupid!
3. shine.
4. Yes, he said, "Be careful!"

Contrasting Pairs 22 – page 105

1. Not the dark one.
2. You can drive it.
3. in the trash can.
4. No, a thief took it.

Contrasting Pairs 23 – page 106

1. That's too bad!
2. I have a son."
3. With a "J."
4. I only eat egg whites.

Contrasting Pairs 24 – page 107

1. of the business profits.
2. Yes. Eat your food.
3. It's dirty.
4. one is mine?"

Syllable Stress Flash Cards

Syllable Stress Flash Cards

Directions

Cut a page of Syllable Stress Flash Cards into individual cards. Working alone or with a partner or group, sort the cards into the correct boxes in the Matching Chart on page 112.

Check your answers with a dictionary or the teacher. Then mark the stressed syllable in each word with an accent mark (') and practice pronouncing each word with your group. Keep your vocabulary words on a ring or in a clear plastic bag for individual review and practice.

Example: *Nationalities*

● ·	· ●	● · ·
GERMAN	**CHINESE**	**MEXICAN**
· ● ·	· · ●	● · · ·
BRAZILIAN	**JAPANESE**	**LIECHTENSTEINER**
· ● · ·	· · ● ·	· · · ●
AMERICAN	**GUATEMALAN**	**VIETNAMESE**

Syllable Stress Flash Cards

Matching Chart

● ·	· ●	● · ·
· ● ·	· · ●	● · · ·
· ● · ·	· · ● ·	· · · ●

Syllable Stress Flash Cards

Conversation

Answers page 124

AGREE	ANSWER	APOLOGIZE
ARGUE	COMMUNICATE	DESCRIBE
DISCUSS	EXPLAIN	LISTEN
PROMISE	PRONOUNCE	SUGGEST
ARGUMENT	DISCUSSION	INTERRUPT

Syllable Stress Flash Cards

Geography

Answers page 124

CAPITAL	CITY	COUNTRY
CULTURE	EUROPE	LOCAL
MOUNTAIN	POPULATION	REGION
UNITED	CANAL	WASHINGTON
AGRICULTURE	TERRITORY	ENVIRONMENT

Syllable Stress Flash Cards

Health

Answers page 125

ADVISE	ALCOHOL	CONDITION
DIET	DOCTOR	EMERGENCY
EXERCISE	HEALTHY	HOSPITAL
PATIENT	SICKNESS	VEGETABLES
DIAGNOSE	SANITARY	OPERATION

Syllable Stress Flash Cards

Leisure

Answers page 125

CELEBRATION	IMAGINE	INVITE
MAGAZINE	MUSIC	QUIET
RELAX	TELEVISION	THEATER
TOGETHER	TRAVEL	VISIT
EXERCISES	ACTIVITIES	RECREATION

Syllable Stress Flash Cards

-LY Words

Answers page 126

ACTUALLY	COSTLY	ESPECIALLY
EASILY	FINALLY	LATELY
SLOWLY	PROBABLY	QUICKLY
REALLY	SUDDENLY	USUALLY
QUIETLY	IMPOLITELY	CORRECTLY

Syllable Stress Flash Cards

Money and Shopping

Answers page 126

AMOUNT	BORROW	BUDGET
DOLLAR	EXPENSIVE	SALARY
MONEY	PURCHASE	RETURN
GUARANTEE	VALUE	WAGES
VALUABLE	COMPARISON	ECONOMICS

Syllable Stress Flash Cards

People

Answers page 127

CITIZEN	COMMUNITY	DAUGHTER
GRANDFATHER	HUSBAND	MAJORITY
MOTHER	MR. (MISTER)	MYSELF
NOBODY	PERSON	POPULATION
DESCENDANTS	PERSONNEL	ANYBODY

Syllable Stress Flash Cards

School

Answers page 127

COLLEGE	EDUCATION	INFORMATION
INTELLIGENT	KNOWLEDGE	PARAGRAPH
PERIOD	REMEMBER	STUDY
SUCCEED	TEACHER	UNDERSTAND
TUITION	KINDERGARTEN	ACADEMY

Syllable Stress Flash Cards

Time

Answers page 128

AGO	ALREADY	ALWAYS
BEGIN	CENTURY	O'CLOCK
SOMETIME	SUDDENLY	TOMORROW
TONIGHT	UNTIL	YESTERDAY
PUNCTUALLY	HISTORICAL	HESITATION

Syllable Stress Flash Cards

Travel

Answers page 128

AIRPLANE	SECURITY	HELICOPTER
PEDESTRIAN	SUBWAY	MOTEL
DISEMBARK	AUTOMOBILE	GARAGE
RESERVATION	MOTORCYCLE	INTERSTATE
ROUNDABOUT	DEPARTURE	TERMINAL

Syllable Stress Flash Cards

Work

Answers page 129

APPLY	BUSINESS	COMPANY
EMPLOY	EQUIPMENT	EXPERIENCE
MANAGE	ORGANIZE	PRESIDENT
RESPONSIBLE	TELEPHONE	WAGES
VOLUNTEER	OPERATOR	OCCUPATION

Syllable Stress Flash Cards

ANSWER KEY

GEOGRAPHY p 114

CAP I TAL
WASH ING TON

AG RI CUL TURE
TER RI TOR Y

CA NAL

POP U LA TION

CIT Y
COUN TRY
CUL TURE
EU ROPE
LO CAL
MOUN TAIN
RE GION

U NIT ED

EN VI RON MENT

CONVERSATION p 113

AR GU MENT

A GREE
DE SCRIBE
DIS CUSS
EX PLAIN
PRO NOUNCE
SUG GEST

IN TER RUPT

AN SWER
AR GUE
LIS TEN
PROM ISE

DIS CUS SION

A POL O GIZE
COM MU NI CATE

Syllable Stress Flash Cards

ANSWER KEY

HEALTH p 115

DI ET
DOC TOR
HEALTH Y
PA TIENT
SICK NESS

AD VISE

AL CO HOL
EX ER CISE
HOS PI TAL
VEGE TA BLES

CON DI TION

DI AG NOSE

SAN I TAR Y

E MER GEN CY

OP ER A TION

LEISURE p 116

MU SIC
QUI ET
TRAV EL
VIS IT

IN VITE
RE LAX

MAG A ZINE*
THE A TER

IM AG INE
TO GETH ER

MAG A ZINE*

EX ER CIS ES
TEL E VI SION

AC TIV I TIES

CEL E BRA TION
REC RE A TION

* Magazine can be pronounced in two ways.

Syllable Stress Flash Cards

ANSWER KEY

MONEY AND SHOPPING p 118

BOR ROW
BUDG ET
DOL LAR
MON EY
PUR CHASE
VAL UE
WA GES

A MOUNT
RE TURN

SAL A RY

EX PEN SIVE

GUAR AN TEE

VAL U A BLE

COM PAR I SON

EC O NOM ICS

-LY WORDS p 117

COST LY
LATE LY
QUICK LY
REAL LY
SLOW LY

EAS I LY
FI NAL LY
PROB A BLY
QUI ET LY
SUD DEN LY

COR RECT LY

AC TU AL LY
U SU AL LY

ES PE CIAL LY

IM PO LITE LY

Syllable Stress Flash Cards

PEOPLE *p 119*

• ● (stress on 1st)	DAUGH TER / HUS BAND / MOTH ER / MR. (MIS TER) / PER SON
● •	MY SELF
● • (stress pattern)	CIT I ZEN / GRAND FA THER / NO BOD Y
● • •	DE SCEN DANTS
• ● •	PER SON NEL
● • • •	AN Y BOD Y
● • • •	COM MU NI TY / MA JOR I TY
• ● • •	POP U LA TION

SCHOOL *p 120*

● •	COL LEGE / KNOWL EDGE / STUD Y / TEACH ER
• ●	SUC CEED
• • ●	PAR A GRAPH / PE RI OD
• ● •	RE MEM BER / TU I TION
● • •	UN DER STAND
• • • ●	KIN DER GAR TEN
● • • •	IN TEL LI GENT / A CAD E MY
• ● • •	ED U CA TION / IN FOR 'MA TION

Syllable Stress Flash Cards

ANSWER KEY

TRAVEL p 122

Stress pattern	Words
● • •	IN TER STATE / ROUND A BOUT / TER MI NAL
● •	MO TEL / GA RAGE
● •	AIR PLANE / SUB WAY
● • • •	MOT OR CY CLE / HEL I COP TER / AUT O MO BILE
• ● •	DIS EM BARK
• ● •	DE PART TURE
• • ● •	RE SER VA TION
• ● • •	PED ES TRI AN / SE CUR I TY

TIME p 121

Stress pattern	Words
● • •	CEN TU RY / SUD DEN LY / YES TER DAY
• ● •	A GO / BE GIN / O' CLOCK / TO NIGHT / UN TIL
● • • •	PUNC TU AL LY
• • ● •	HES I TA TION
● •	AL WAYS / SOME TIME
• ● •	AL READ Y / TO MOR ROW
• ● • •	HI STOR I CAL

Syllable Stress Flash Cards

ANSWER KEY

WORK p 123

BUSI NESS MAN AGE WA GES	AP PLY EM PLOY	COM PA NY OR GAN IZE PRES I DENT TEL E PHONE
E QUIP MENT	VOL UN TEER	OP ER A TOR
EX PE RI ENCE RE SPON SI BLE	OCC U PA TION	

Glossary
of Pronunciation Terms

aspiration: The puff of air that accompanies certain sounds such as /p/, /t/, and /k/. The position of the sound in a word affects the strength of aspiration. For example, the sound /p/ in *pot* has stronger aspiration than the /p/ in *spot* or *top.*

blending (linking): A feature of spoken English that relates to the connecting of words within a thought group. For example, *with–them* and *bus–stop* are pronounced without a break between the words. Also, the phrase *last–time–I–got–on–a–plane* is pronounced with the end of one word linked smoothly to the next.

consonants: One of the two main classes of speech sounds. (The other class is **vowels**.) Consonants are produced with a constriction or closure at some place in the vocal tract. For example, the letters and sounds **m** and **n** in *man* are consonants.

consonant cluster: Two or more adjacent consonant sounds. For example, the sounds and letters **nst** form a final consonant cluster in the word *against.*

diphthong: A combination of a vowel sound and a **semivowel** in a single **syllable**. For example, the /ay/ sound in *light,* the /yu/ sound in *use,* and the /æw/ sound in *out* are diphthongs.

intonation: The musical features of a phrase, including the rise and fall of pitch. For example, the final intonation of *What happened?*↓ is falling but that of *Is it far?*↑ is rising.

reduction: The shortened form of a word or phrase that occurs in normal conversation. It is a spoken form, but is normally not written. Reductions include spoken words such as *wanna (want to), gonna (going to),* and *whaddaya (what do/are you).* These forms are frequent in spoken English and are essential for comprehension of natural conversations.

root (stem): The base, or dictionary, form of a word, without prefixes or suffixes. For example, the root of *laughs* or *laughing* is *laugh.*

schwa: /ə/ The relaxed, neutral vowel similar in sound to "uh." It is the most common vowel sound in spoken English and may be spelled with any of the vowel letters. For example, the **a** in *ago,* the **e** in *gallery,* the **u** and **i** in *punish,* and the **o** in *from* are all pronounced with the schwa sound. The schwa may be **stressed** or unstressed.

semivowel (glide): The short vowel sound forming part of a **diphthong**, and often spelled with the letter **y** or **w**. For example, the **y** in *yes* is a semivowel. (Notice, however, that the **y** in *baby* is not a semivowel because it represents the full vowel sound /i/.)

stress: The characteristic of spoken English that makes one **syllable** in a word or one word in a phrase stronger than the other syllables or words. For example, the syllable *–stand* in *understand* is stressed. The word *loves* in *She loves him* is normally stressed. A stressed syllable or word is pronounced longer, louder, and higher in pitch than the other syllables or words.

syllable: An uninterrupted speech sound or sequence of sounds. It is composed of a vowel sound and may or may not have consonants in front of or after the vowel. For example, *man* has one syllable, *sister* has two syllables, and *united* has three syllables.

voiced: A feature of speech sounds in which the vocal chords are vibrating. All English vowel sounds are voiced. Consonant sounds such as /b/, /m/, /v/, and /z/ are voiced.

voiceless: A feature of speech sounds in which the vocal cords are not vibrating. Consonants such as /p/, /f/, and /s/ are voiceless.

vowels: One of the two main classes of speech sounds. (The other class is **consonants**.) Vowels are produced with an open vocal tract, with vibration of the vocal cords. For example, the letter **a** /æ/ in *man* is a vowel.

Other Pro Lingua pronunciation books

From Sound to Sentence. A Basic and fun literacy and spelling workbook based on a phonics approach supplemented by sight words. From *Pat's pet bat* to *the lazy zebra* and *the crazy ox*. Supplemented with three CDs.

Superphonic Bingo. 15 photocopyable games following the presentation of sound-letter combinations in *From Sound to Sentence*. Each game has 8 different cards and two incomplete cards.

Rhymes 'n Rhythms. Your students will enjoy the choral work in these 32 rhythmic rhymes that develop the student's ability to speak with English stress, rhythm, and intonation. A CD is also available for use with this photocopyable text.

Teaching North American English Pronunciation. There are two parts to this book. Part One, for the teacher, is a brief introduction to English phonology including the suprasegmental system of stress, intonation, rhythm and linking. Part Two is a collection of photocopyable handouts to be used with learners. Three CDs are available.

Pronunciation Activities: Vowels in Limericks. 16 comical limericks present the basic vowels of English. Each limerick is followed by a variety of pronunciation and sound-letter correspondence activities. CD available.

A-Z Picture Activities: Phonics and Vocabulary for Emerging Readers. The units in the book proceed through the alphabet letter by letter. Each unit is fully illustrated with key vocabulary pages, and phonics pages with short exercises illustrate words with different spellings and the same sound. The pictures are lively and engaging. A CD pronounces the words in the illustrations.

Stress Rulz! Pronunciation through Rap (Book and CD). Teach the rules of stress in English with rap. The raps move progressively from syllable to sentence stress. The students listen and then perform.

Pronunciation Card Games. Photocopyable. Copy, cut out, and paste the games onto index cards. The games involve minimal pairs, emphatic stress, syllabification, and stress placement.

Questions? Simply give us a call, and we'll try to help.
800-366-4775 • 802-257-7779
Webstore: www.ProLinguaAssociates.com